REDISCOVERING HOPE

OUR GREATEST TEACHING STRATEGY

RICHARD L. CURWIN

NATIONAL EDUCATIONAL SERVICE
BLOOMINGTON, INDIANA   1992

Copyright © 1992 by National Educational Service
304 West Kirkwood Avenue, Suite 2
Bloomington, Indiana 47404-5132
(812) 336-7700
(800) 733-6786 (toll-free)
FAX: (812) 336-7790
e-mail: nes@nesonline.com
www.nesonline.com

Cover design by Joe La Mantia

Printed in the United States of America

Printed on recycled paper

ISBN 1-879639-24-6

About the Author

*Don't let life discourage you; everyone who got
where he is had to begin where he was.*

RICHARD L. CURWIN, ED.D.,
is the co-author of
*Discovering Your Teaching
Self, Discipline with Dignity, Am I in
Trouble: Using Discipline to Teach
Young Children Responsibility,* and
*Developing Responsibility and
Self-Discipline.* In addition, Dr.
Curwin has written articles that
have appeared in *Educational
Leadership, Instructor, Learning,* and
other education journals. He has taught at both the junior
high school and university levels. His concern for the
well-being of children has been the driving force in his writ-
ing, inservice training, and teaching. He credits most of this
understanding of children to his three sons: David, Andrew,
and Danny.

Dedication

THIS BOOK IS DEDICATED TO THE STUDENTS who sit in the back of the room, to help them find the courage to dream and to help them find the strength and commitment to make their dreams come true.

This book is also dedicated to the wonderful teachers who keep searching for the keys, any keys, to unlock the doors that hold those dreams. They hold tight to their ideals even while spending much of their professional lives beating their heads against a wall, or so it often seems. I hope they see that their efforts, individually and collectively, actually move that wall. The students in the back of the room cannot make it without them.

And to a master locksmith, Raymond Wlodkowski. He has taught me the meaning of educational motivation and how it translates into hope. His standards are uncompromisingly high, as is his dedication to meeting them. Schools, teachers, students, and I have greatly benefited from such standards and dedication.

Acknowledgments

Special thanks...

...to my dear colleague and friend, Allen Mendler, who not only co-developed the Discipline with Dignity program (from which so many of the ideas in this book were derived), but who also is always there for me with support and love when my own ability to be hopeful is challenged.

...to Phil Harris, who exemplifies dignity, grace, professionalism, and caring for all those who have the good fortune to know him.

I gratefully acknowledge the support, ideas, and the many opportunities to learn provided by the following people: Raymond Wlodkowski, Steve Sanborn, Chuck Knisley, Alan Blankstein, Nancy Shin, Andrew Curwin, Danny Curwin, David Curwin, Otis Dehann Carlyle, Gretchen Kocinsky, Jane Mason, Claire Taylor, Patty Simons, Bernard Palmer, Barbara Fuhrmann, Patrick DeMarte, Robert Prague, and Gordon Cawelti. I also wish to thank the Texas Elementary Principals Association, and the many educators who have helped me over the years, including teachers and administrators in Chittlin County, Vermont; the Appalachian School District in Newfoundland; the Step schools in Kansas City; Marcia Cooper and the teachers and administrators at Stephen S. Wise Temple Elementary and Community Middle/High Schools in Los Angeles; Ann Timm and the teachers and administrators from Flint, Michigan. Also deserving special thanks are the participants in the "Discipline with Dignity" training series sponsored by Phi Delta Kappa and my seventh-grade class at Granby Junior Senior High School in 1969.

Table of Contents

Preface

The last question the principal asked me during my job interview was, "Can you teach hard-to-motivate kids?" I answered confidently, "Of course. That is one of my greatest strengths." Back in the late Sixties, teaching positions in English were rare; so if he had asked me if I could motivate comatose kids, I would have said, "Of course. That is one of my greatest strengths." I was so happy to get the job, I did not ask what he meant by "hard-to-motivate."

My class consisted of ten seventh-grade boys who were considered by everyone to be the dregs of the school. No other teacher wanted them, so the principal put them in an isolated, self-contained class; and he hoped he would never hear from them or from me until June.

I spent most of the month before school developing learning activities for hard-to-motivate seventh-graders. I asked everyone I knew how they would motivate "hard-to-motivate" kids. The mood of the Sixties influenced most of the answers, which ranged from blowing up the school, to sharing my feelings so they could feel good about me, to relating to them with all levels of my inner consciousness.

I was more comfortable designing motivating classroom games. I made felt board games to teach vocabulary and baseball games to teach math. I had Jeopardy-type games to teach social studies and "Mad scientist" games for science. I figured everybody loves to play games. The boys would have so much fun that they would not even know they were learning.

The day before the kids came, I took my three boxes of games and set out to prepare my classroom. I was full of energy and hope. Ideas buzzed around my brain like bees around a hive. Sadly, I never had a chance to use any of my games. On the morning of the first day, one of my students stole his father's car and drove it to school. He was 14 years old. The principal, in a state of panic, immediately called me to the office. "Get that kid and that car out of here," he shouted. "I don't want the police and the newspapers here on the first day of school."

By the time I got back to my room, the other boys had found the boxes and made confetti out of them. The trashed games were a perfect metaphor for the entire year. I eventually had to trash all of my preconceived plans and concepts of how to motivate "hard-to-motivate" kids.

Their problems were severe. During the course of the year, one boy tried to hang himself in the coat closet and nearly succeeded, two got arrested, and all of us were thrown out of a zoo by an irate zookeeper who threatened to let the animals out of the cages and lock my class in. Police had to be called into the planetarium because two of my boys almost managed to remove the main lens during a light show. I developed headaches, severe stomach disorders, and a strong desire to apply to graduate school for the following year.

My students taught me the true meaning of "at risk," a term that had not yet been invented. For that entire year, I was a teacher at risk. I also learned some important lessons about students who are "hard-to-motivate." I learned that all my expectations of how things would affect them were guesses at best and foolish at worst. For the last 15 years, I have focused most of my professional life on the issue of "discipline." If I were to summarize what I have learned in those 15 years, I would say something that anyone who works with children already knows well: Most techniques for behavior management work best for the kids who do not need them, and it is extremely difficult to find techniques that consistently work for those kids who need them most. The most difficult students are those who no longer care, those who have lost hope for their future both in school and in life.

I also learned that I had to let go of my ideas of what a teacher was and did; what a school was and how it should function. Since no method or procedure typically used in school had worked with these kids, I had to find new ones or continue to fail. I came to understand the theory of holes that says, "when you are in one, stop digging." And I learned that all kids, even those who make serious attempts at suicide, have dreams and hopes about their future. They all prefer to be successful in school and feel genuine joy when they learn and master something new. They also are reachable at least some of the time, want to be liked and respected by teachers, and deserve the best chance that we can give them.

THEY'RE STILL HERE

During a visit to Tokyo, I had the opportunity to visit a large junior-senior high school and chat, with the aid of an interpreter (who was also an educator), with the principal and assistant principal. I asked many questions about how they dealt with students who were discipline problems with little success in eliciting an answer. When I changed my focus to motivation, I was more successful. "What do you do with students who don't want to learn?" I asked. "They're not here anymore," was the reply. "Where are they?" I asked. "We don't know," was the answer.

In America, students who are removed from the classroom always seem to come back (at least until some decide to quit). And the time interval is far too short for the beleaguered teacher who removed them. This book is written with the hope of not only keeping them here, but for helping them to learn during their stay. And for minimizing the sense of relief when they are absent by changing the nature of their relationship with those around them.

Ellen Goodman of the *Boston Globe* once defined insanity as "continuing to do the same thing expecting different results." It is insane to think that simply by doing more of the same things, we can positively influence "hard-to-motivate" students. Hope intrinsically means desire for change for the better. Change will only occur with the courage and commitment to stop doing what we are doing, and start doing something else.

WHAT DOES "AT RISK" MEAN AND HOW DO I USE IT?

Nicholson looked up at him, and sustained the look — detaining him. "What would you do if you could change the educational system?"....

*"Well...I'm not too sure what I'd do," Teddy said. "I know I'm pretty sure I wouldn't start with the things schools usually start with." He folded his arms and reflected briefly. "I think I'd first just assemble all the children together and **show them how to find out who they are,** not just **what** their names are and things like that...I guess, even before that, I'd get them to empty out everything their parents and everybody ever told them. I mean even if their parents just told them an elephant's big, I'd make them empty that out. An elephant's only big when it's next to some-*

*thing else — a dog or a lady, for example." Teddy thought another moment. "I wouldn't even tell them an elephant has a trunk. I might **show** them an elephant, if I had one handy, but I'd let them just walk up to the elephant, not knowing anything more about it than the **elephant knew about them.** The same thing with grass, and other things. I wouldn't even tell them grass is green. Colors are only names. I mean if you tell them the grass is green it makes them start expecting the grass to look a certain way — your way — instead of some other way that may be just as good, and maybe much better...I don't know. I'd just make them vomit up every bit of the apple their parents and everybody made them take a bite out of."*[1]

Care must be taken when using labels with children. Terms such as "at risk" are best used to identify special needs and services, not to predetermine abilities or achievement. They are not helpful as explanations of why a child does something: "He is constantly out of his seat because he is emotionally disordered," or "He doesn't do his homework because he is at risk." Used in this manner, labels are misleading and block deeper investigation into what motivates the student's behavior and what the student truly needs. Students often live up to or down to the expectations of their labels, even though the labels are inaccurate, incomplete, or unfair.

This book is about "students at risk." This is another label. It makes for more efficient communication, but it limits perception. I twinge a little every time I use that expression, but I was not wise or clever enough to write this book without it. I have tried to use the "at risk" label diagnostically, as a description of a set of circumstances rather than as a judgment of character.

It is what students do under the conditions they are in, not who they are, that puts them at risk. Generally, for one reason or another, they have stopped learning, have stopped caring, have stopped believing that school will make a positive difference in their lives. They accept the limits others have given them.

More than discipline techniques are needed for these students. They need hope. The purpose of this book is to give hope to students who have lost it: first by understanding how hope was lost, then by suggesting both schoolwide and classroom changes to bring it back. Without hope, nothing else we attempt will matter. Students without hope put us all "at risk."

It is also easy to label all schools as inadequate and all teachers as unable to handle the at risk student, mired in unfeeling lectures, caught up in outmoded grading systems, and helplessly throwing up their hands in despair. This is far from the truth. There are many exemplary schools throughout the United States that reach the student at risk. There are many teachers who expertly change the perceptions of these students from hopelessness to believing in themselves. If you ask at risk students who their favorite teachers are, they always have an answer, and those teachers have found the key to unlock the door that separates the at risk learner from his more successful peers.

AT RISK STUDENTS AND MINORITIES

Minority students comprise the majority of students at risk. African-American males are literally an endangered species in America. The largest growing minority in America are the Hispanics, who are even less noticed by the bureaucracies than are African-Americans. Minority children need special services at the youngest ages possible, especially programs like Head Start. The strategies and suggestions in this volume are not written only for minority children. These are generic suggestions for all children who have lost their hope for learning. At risk children come in all sizes, colors, and flavors, and speak a variety of languages and dialects. They come from both impoverished and advantaged homes and from parents who might abuse them or care deeply about them. Every individual in school who feels hopeless deserves the opportunity to renew their feelings of hope. This book is for all of them.

IS THERE REALLY HOPE?

Gathering information for this book was, at times, very discouraging. The picture appears rather gloomy when all the problems facing children are pieced together. As the Phi Delta Kappa Study of At Risk Students clearly shows, the number and severity of social ills is overwhelming. I asked Jack Frymier, the author of the study, if he still had hope after working on this project. He was very hopeful, enthusiastic, and positive that schools can and should make a significant difference in what happens to these children. "Heart attacks are caused mostly by factors related to heredity, which are not controllable," he said. "Yet doctors do not give up. They do as much as possible to understand what they can't change and manipulate what they can. The result has been vast improvements in both the frequency and treatment of heart attacks. Educators can do the same."

Of course there is hope. Schools cannot cure all the evils of society. Schools might not be able to guarantee a successful future for all students. But schools can, at the minimum, provide an oasis for those children who desperately need one. The school may be the only place where all children are treated

with dignity, where they learn to behave responsibly and discover the magic of learning. Educators must put forth the
effort.

We can even hope for more. Not every student will succeed, but many can. Each of their lives is important and worth
fighting for. Schools can become the opposite of our throwaway society, a place where every individual matters. As Jack
Frymier said, "Let's get going."

---

1. Salinger, J. D. "Teddy," *Nine Stories,* (New York: Bantam,
   1953), 195-196.

WRITTEN IN MATH CLASS

I sit here in my prison cell,
With its malodorous prison smell.
They always ask me what I've learned.
I tell them "nothing." They get burned.

Escape is easy if I try,
But if I succeed, I'll surely die.
With a section two feet wide,
Surrounded by myself on every side.

I wonder. I think. I comprehend.
Will my sentence ever end?
Eleven years down and one to go.
It's all an act; it's all a show.

"Brutality," is what I cry,
As the wardens waddle by.
I've done no crime. Why am I here?
I believe it's to better me, and give me fear.

They don't answer, don't inform.
They just pressure me to conform.
If I do badly I'll stay longer.
Which makes my feelings even stronger.

To keep me here that's their only goal.
You can have my body but not my soul.

— Andrew Steven Curwin
A Junior at Brighton High School
Rochester, NY

One

The Seed Is Planted

*Don't let life discourage you; everyone who got
where he is had to begin where he was.*

— Richard L. Evans

IMAGINE ENTERING A LARGE SUPERMARKET. You are
approached by the manager, who says with a scowl on his
face, "If you intend to shop in this store, you might try
wearing some decent clothes. A little soap wouldn't hurt either.
This is a store, not a playground."

A short time later, you ask a clerk where a new kind of
sauce might be found. He says belligerently, "Everybody else
knows where it is; what's wrong with you? Maybe if you came
a little earlier and looked around, you wouldn't be bothering
me with stupid questions."

At the checkout counter, you discover that you only have
$100, but the bill comes to $110. As you pick out $10 worth of
items to return, the cashier announces on the loudspeaker,
"Another shopper who can't do basic math."

Undoubtedly, you would not return to that store, at least
not to shop. But what if you were required to shop at that
store, by law, 180 days a year? You would be called, "a shopper

at risk." There would be a special section of the store where you would be assigned to shop, and the staff would have inservice training to learn how to handle shoppers like you.

There are many factors that place students at risk, but in school the seed is planted the first time they feel unwelcome. It begins with an attack on their dignity, or when they sense that other students are valued or appreciated more than they are. It happens the first time they notice a derogatory label applied to them.

Eventually, the seed grows into cynicism: "What's the use? No matter how hard I try, I'm not good enough." Attacks on dignity erode the student's hope for success. Without hope, there is simply no reason to try.

Students at risk accept their experiences and perceptions as truth. They become hardened and unreachable. These students learn that it feels better to be bad than it does to be stupid, so their behavior worsens. The school responds by rejecting them even more.

High risk students are like vacuum cleaners, sucking up our time, energy, and resources. Many educators wonder why they have to put up with disruptive students: "If they aren't interested in learning, then I'm not interested in teaching them." Ironically, these educators feel much as do the high risk students. They feel labeled, wronged, angry, protective, alienated, and above all, hopeless. There is nothing that can be done to improve the situation.

Teachers speak to the "good kids" with different facial expressions and tones of voice than they use for the high risk students. Good kids are called on more often and given more chances to demonstrate responsible behavior. But our responsibility, both as professionals and as caretakers of children, is to educate all the children who enter the school, not just the good ones. This is hard to remember during the day-to-day struggle to teach. It is not an easy job. But students at risk need an education as much as, if not more than, the children who are easier to teach. As a society, we can no longer afford children who do not learn. We must find a way to teach all the kids we get in our classrooms, including those we choose to label "high risk."

Allen Mendler and I began our book, *Discipline With Dignity*,[1] by asking the question, "Who are schools for?" We ended the book by answering: "Schools are for kids, all kids." They are our clients, and we are the professionals there to meet their educational needs.

For the schools to reach and teach high risk students, a massive dose of hope must be infused into every school, every classroom, and every teacher. Cynicism is just as dangerous to educators as it is to children. If we write these kids off, then they are truly without hope.

One of the most important lessons on reaching and motivating children was taught to me by my youngest son, Danny. When he was 12 years old, Danny was hit by a truck while riding his bicycle. He was seriously hurt, and for a while we did not know whether he would live. He totally recovered and was soon back on his feet, but it took me much longer to recover. I couldn't work for months after Danny was back in school.

Around that time, Raymond Wlodkowski invited me to help with a workshop in Newpoort, Belgium, for Department of Defense European school administrators. The workshop was to be held the next fall, and Raymond and I agreed to spend a weekend in London before traveling to Belgium. I planned to take Danny to London with me for a week before meeting Raymond. After Danny's accident, this trip became one of the most important events in the world to me.

The summer before the trip, Danny told me he had something very important to ask me. When I asked him what he wanted, he said it was private and we needed to be alone. Safe in my room with the door closed, Danny said, "Promise that no matter what I do this summer, I still get to go to London."

I responded quickly, "Of course you are going to London. This trip means more to me than you can ever realize, and nothing could stop me from taking you."

He said, "Okay, thanks," and headed for the door. I stopped him and asked how he could ever conceive of a question like that.

"Because I know you," he explained.

"What do you mean by that?"

"I mean that if you get mad at me, I know what you will say. 'Danny, if you don't clean your room, you can't go to London. Danny, if you don't put the computer games away, you can't go to London.' And then the biggie, 'Danny, if you don't stop fighting with your brothers, you can't go to London.'" Then he said in a calm, rational voice, "Daddy, I don't care if you say those things. You can threaten all you want, as long as I know you don't mean them. I don't want to spend the whole summer worrying about the trip, because I really want to go."

Danny taught me one of the most powerful lessons about children I have ever learned. They can behave and "be good" for 95% of the time; but if they screw up even that 5%, then they might lose something they love.

What would Danny's behavior have been that summer if we had not had that talk and I used one of the threats he accurately predicted I might use? He might have lost hope for a most-cherished activity. I would have lost all leverage to reach him, and his behavior would have worsened, not improved.

We simply cannot expect children to be angels and then take their hope away when they behave like children instead. It is just as important to acknowledge the 95% or 80% or even 10% of the time when they can behave or perform the way we demand, as it is to criticize and blame when they do not. The more we focus on the negative, the more cynical and jaded children become.

Cynicism is contagious, but so is hopefulness. This book is about hope: How to give the turned-off student hope to succeed. Just as important, it is about giving educators hope to succeed with "hopeless" students. The ideas in this book are based on the beliefs that things change and, especially, that things can improve. Maybe not every idea can work; but if we do not try, nothing will get better. If we keep using the same methods, we will continue to get the same results, and that simply is not good enough.

---

1. Curwin, Richard, and Mendler, Allen, *Discipline with Dignity* (Alexandria, VA: ASCD, 1988).

Two

A Society at Risk: Children without Hope

Education is in the headlines again. After years of shameful neglect, educators and politicians have taken the pulse of the public school and found it faint. Concern for the health of public education, stirred by a spate of new studies, offers fresh hope that in the years ahead we'll be able to adopt a serious, coherent plan for school reform. Getting the public's attention always has been the first step in the march toward progress in our nation.

— Ernest L. Boyer

HIGH SCHOOL: A REPORT ON SECONDARY EDUCATION IN AMERICA

Recently I asked a large number of teachers to describe the characteristics of students whom they would label "high risk." Some teachers said "lazy, turned off, bored." Others said, "unable to reach their full potential," or "angry, hostile, and anti-social." Many felt that the high risk student was the potential dropout. Descriptions such as irresponsible, alienated, unmotivated, suffering emotionally, low skill development, disruptive, withdrawn, dislikes school, has an "attitude," learning deficient, and agitated were mentioned frequently.

The Phi Delta Kappa Study of Students At Risk says that "children are high risk if they are likely to fail either in school or in life."[1] After giving that definition to the teachers, I followed up with this question: "Is it possible that every student in the United States is potentially high risk?" The answer from every teacher was a resounding "yes."

Does this mean that all students fit the bleak description above? I do not think so. When examined carefully, the descriptions listed above are symptoms of hopeless people. The central characteristic of a student at risk is either the potential or actual loss of hope. Without hope for success, students do not care.

Why does it seem that every student in America has the potential to lose hope for success? Why does it seem that more students than ever before do not care about school or about their education? Not long ago, such reports as *A Nation at Risk* blamed our nation's schools. However, it is difficult to separate why schools are failing from the larger question of why our society is failing.

In a world with instant communication and easy access to information, it is naive to believe that students are not affected by the larger world around them. Television, movies, and news media react so quickly to local and world events that our youth digest significant cultural phenomena by the time they digest their fast-food hamburgers. Not only are wars fought on television like video games, but they become video games within days of their outbreak. Earthquake T-shirts were sold the day after the Prima Loma earthquake in San Francisco in 1989. Saddam dolls designed for mutilation were sold within a week of the first Desert Storm air attacks. Movie scripts are developed based on events as they are happening.

Students internalize the many images that flash past their eyes as definitive statements of reality. They do not have much time to think about these images or to evaluate what they mean. New ones come along too quickly for that. The perceptions students compose are rapidly changing mosaics comprised of sound bites and media interpretations of what is going on all around them. The resulting "picture" is not pretty. Students are reminded over and over again of their relative worth and what the future has in store for them. The following conditions not only negatively affect children, but also strongly influence the way children behave in school and how we must adapt to teach them.

1. The basic family unit is not providing what children need for emotional, social, and intellectual security.

The basic family unit has been consistently unstable for the past 20 years. In the last 10 years, approximately 2.5 million adults have had their parents get divorced. In 1990, 2.4 million marriages were remarriages for at least one partner. And 60% of these remarriages will end in divorce.[2]

As more parents are unable to care for their children, grandparents are becoming surrogate parents. According to the U.S. Census Bureau, 3 million children live with their grandparents, a jump of 50% over the last decade.[3]

The destabilization of the family has made it difficult for children to feel that their world is predictable and controllable. The family is the strongest safety net children have when the world around them is full of danger. As this safety net deteriorates, so do feelings of stability and certainty. Recent studies of children of divorce indicate that their suffering continues well into adult life.[4] While every divorce is not necessarily bad, and many are for the best, the vast numbers of them indicate to children at a cultural level that quitting is as acceptable as trying to work things out, and that the sanctity of the family is not immune to danger.

The toll on children living in unstable families is horrifying. A report prepared last year by the Institute of Medicine estimates that as many as 7.5 million children, 12% of the under-eighteen population, suffer from some form of psychological illness. The sad truth is that a growing number of American youngsters have home lives that are hostile to emotional growth. Psyches are extremely fragile and must be nourished from birth. Everyone starts out with a basic anxiety about survival. An attentive parent contains that stress by making the child feel secure and loved.[5]

2. The influence of the Media is increasing.

Children spend too much time watching television and the rate is increasing. Newton Minow, the director of Annenberg Washington Program in Communications Policy Studies, says:

> *Television is not a tool for nurturing. It is a tool for selling. Television fails our children. And it fails them for more hours each day than they spend with a teacher in a classroom.*[6]
> *Commercial television has even infiltrated the school day. For example, Channel One offers schools free equipment and news service in exchange for requiring students to view two minutes of commercials each day.*

The main message of commercial television is that personal worth is measured by what you own, not by what you do. You can get dates, respect, and self-worth if you drive a certain car, drink a certain beer, have a certain look, own a certain appliance, or use a certain soap. Because self-esteem based on such trivial things does not last very long, television teaches children to continually wonder if they have worth at all.

When children are constantly pitched to by advertisers, even in schools, they soon realize that they are valued in society only as consumers. As long as they buy, they have worth. Implicit is the message that success in school translates to getting a job so that consumer goods can be purchased. If there are faster ways to make money, like selling drugs, their bodies (sports, the armed forces, or prostitution), or their souls, why not? As long as they have the right athletic shoes, they will be successful.

3. Children are not safe.

They are going hungry, according to a report by the Washington-based Food Research and Action Center. "One in eight children under the age of 12 years old—5.5 million kids—goes hungry each day."[7]

For some children, the danger is more acute. Children have been robbed and even killed for their clothes, especially their sneakers. Advertisements make certain products so attractive that those who do not have the money to purchase them are willing to do whatever it takes to get them, even commit murder. What is most frightening is how easily students accept this bizarre behavior as normal.

4. The number of babies born with alcohol and/or crack cocaine addiction is increasing.

The rapid growth in the number of addicted babies is frightening. Their symptoms include irritability, inability to concentrate, aggressive social behavior, violent outbursts, and little, if any, inner control. A large number of these children will soon be entering our schools.

The national response to pregnant addicts and alcohol abusers leans toward punishment, and some so-called experts have gone so far as to suggest jail terms for addicted mothers. Doctors are fearful that the risk of prison will deter substance-abusing pregnant women from seeking prenatal care, making the problems worse. The creation of treatment centers has been painfully slow, and there are long waiting lists for the treatment centers that do exist.

5. Violence is increasing.

The United States is the most violent of all civilized countries. The number of murders with guns hit an all-time high of 23,220 in 1990—an 8% increase over 1989. The United States leads all other nations in homicides and violent crime, and the vast majority of these crimes are committed by people who personally know their victims. In April, 1991, *Newsweek* reported that, on an average day in America, 1991, 10 children under 18 years old are killed with handguns.[8] In many major cities, children are advised not to stand near open windows in order to avoid stray bullets. In recent history, the United States has used military solutions to solve problems in Grenada, Panama, and the Middle East. Regardless of the political interpretation of the use of military force, the conclusion reached by children is that Rambo-style solutions are preferable to working things out through negotiation. Even Bart Simpson impresses on young minds that sarcasm and fighting are preferable to resolving conflicts through conversation. The more that violence becomes the national standard for solving problems, the more children think that fighting, shooting, and stabbing are legitimate methods for solving their problems.

6. Racial tension is increasing.

On college campuses and in society as a whole, racial tensions are re-emerging. From Massachusetts to Mississippi to New York, the news once again is that racial strife is alive and well. Since most high risk students come from minority backgrounds, they cannot help but wonder whether they are welcome in mainstream society.

Hate organizations like the New Aryan Nation are growing and drawing membership from young, disconnected, alienated youth. Hate crimes are increasing, ranging from painting swastikas on cemetery markers to murder. The FBI has increased its concern while, at the same time, our government considers whether crimes of hate are legal under the First Amendment.

The minimal national outrage and relative apathy of the population about hate crimes affects those children who notice. They see others express hateful attitudes by blaming, hurting, striking, name calling, or intimidating. In the context of other societal conditions, these attitudes can appear attractive to alienated, hopeless children.

7. Young African-American men are in jeopardy.

A *USA Today* article points out that young African-American men, probably the largest segment of the high risk population, are an endangered species. Twenty-five percent of African-American males between the ages of 23 to 29 are in prison, on parole, or on probation; the estimated number is 609,690, which is substantially higher than the number of

African-American men enrolled in institutions of higher education. Homicide is the leading cause of death for African-American males between ages 15 and 24. The homicide rate for African-American men between the ages of 20 and 29 is six times higher than the rate for the rest of the population at that age. Forty percent of all adult African-American males are functionally illiterate. Life expectancy for African-American males is 65.2 years; for white males it is 72.2 years.[9]

8. The rich are getting richer and the poor are getting poorer.

Many families that once were considered middle class are rapidly joining the ranks of the poor. Two-income families have become a necessity. Low-skilled workers are rapidly finding themselves out of the high-tech job market.

> *The change occurred in 1972, when the average, inflation-adjusted weekly wage of American workers reached, in 1982 dollars, $315.44. That was the peak. Since then the decline has been relentless....By the end of 1990, following the largest peacetime economic expansion of the twentieth century, the average wage hit $258.10, the lowest amount since the fifties, an eighteen percent drop.*[10]

Too many children live in poverty. Of the 3.6 million students who entered school in 1991, 25% live in poverty. Fifty percent of African-American and 40% of Hispanic children live in poverty. Out of 80 million U.S. households in 1991, 9.5 million are headed by a single female parent, of whom 16% are under the age 25 and 50% are unemployed.[11]

A growing number of teenagers work up to 40 hours a week. While some work to support cars, others work to buy food for their families. Too many teenagers, when they peer into their future, see burger-flipping or no work at all. It becomes increasingly difficult to use the promise of good jobs as motivation to do well or to stay in school. Even the "slowest" of students clearly see the emptiness of that promise. Many students do see an alternative in crime. When poor youth turn to fast money, they feel little need for an education.

I was waiting in a principal's office in a school at Hunter's Point, a relatively run-down San Francisco neighborhood, when a third-grade girl ran into the waiting area, crying because her lunch money was stolen. One of her classmates, in a very generous moment, opened his wallet and pulled out a roll of $100 bills. He peeled one off and gave it to the little girl. "This should cover it," he said. I was deeply touched by the generosity and sharing demonstrated by this child, but equally concerned about where he got that kind of money. I wondered for the remainder of the day how important his English and math classes were to him, and what he might be thinking when his teacher said such things as, "You need a good education if you are going to get ahead in this world."

9. There is not enough money spent on education.

When President Bush sent our troops into the war in the Persian Gulf, he proclaimed that he would not allow our soldiers to fight with one hand tied behind their backs. But American teachers enter the classroom with both hands tied behind their backs. Budget cuts in nearly every state have caused massive hemorrhaging in school programming, supplies, and support. Politicians insist that throwing money at schools will not solve education's problems. How do they know? It's never been tried. If they know how to buy computers, copy machines without use restrictions, supplies, additional teachers, books, planning time, or media equipment without money, then maybe they're correct. Schools in Richmond, California, were closed on April 28, 1991, because school funds ran out. It took a court order to reopen the schools, an action that was fought by Governor Wilson, who did not want to set a precedent of the state bailing out irresponsible city governments. School closings, increased class size, and budget cuts in education have become business as usual and no longer constitute news.

Financial support for such educational programs as art, music, home economics, and drama is being reduced or cut. These cuts are especially dangerous because a culture defines itself and grows through the arts. Without an understanding of the arts, there can be no true understanding of the values and mores of the culture in which one lives. These cuts reinforce the message that life is not worth much beyond consumerism. Children cannot help noticing that it is more important to the American government to have smart bombs than it is to have smart children.

10. Children are not being heard.

Free expression is eroding. Historically, censorship has been an early sign of cultural and moral decay, forcing a society into one way of thinking. The most likely to be censored are the young and those adults who distribute art created by or for the young. Music stores have been closed and owners arrested for selling explicit rap music. The NRPC, a radical right-wing political group based in Kansas City, is trying to censor rock and roll, the most popular venue American youth has to express itself.

I am not in favor of explicit lyrics; many are repulsive to me. But as a parent I can do far more to restrict what my children listen to and to educate them about wholesome values than can any group of moral police. The danger of political censorship is a far greater threat to our culture than a few explicit, rude lyrics, which can be controlled at the family level.

American parents do not spend enough time interacting with their children. Because we demonstrate the importance of our values by the way we spend our time, the dominant message is that communicating with people is a low priority in our culture. It is hard for children to feel important when no one is willing to find the time to talk to them.

By not listening to our youth, whether or not we like what we might hear, we communicate that we do not care about what they think and what their concerns are. They feel discounted and alienated. The less we listen, the louder they scream. Eventually they will make us notice them whether we care to or not.

These issues are not new. My mother told me that the Beatles and Rolling Stones would rot my brain, just as her mother told her Frank Sinatra would rot her brain. The difference between now and then is that I knew my mother would love me whether my brain was rotting or not. Many children today have no such assurance.

11. Children have fewer heroes, and they no longer have leaders whom they can admire.

The traditional role models have let children down. Sports heroes charge $25 for an autograph and whine when they are offered only a million dollars to play ball for a year; television evangelists are arrested for soliciting prostitutes. Children see their government leaders abusing their privileges by cashing bad checks and using limousines to travel across five states to buy stamps for their collections.

The cumulative effect of these situations on children is the inescapable perception that the world they will inherit is dangerous, unpredictable, and uncaring. There is little to hope for and little to believe in. Children cannot help but feel, in one way or another, that they are not highly valued, that they are more commodities than precious human lives. The image of hopelessness runs through each of these examples like a runaway train.

Is it the fault of the schools that our society has found itself in such dire straits? The "chicken versus the egg" debate has been applied to education: Do breakdowns in society create the decline of the school, or is it the other way around? Most likely they create each other. As one spirals downward, it drags the other with it.

What is most important is to stop blaming and start changing. Schools can become places where hope is rejuvenated for those who have lost it and safeguarded for those who are at risk of losing it in the future.

It is not only the poor and so-called disadvantaged child who is at risk. Many children from upper-middle-class homes who go to the finest schools face a different, yet potent, danger. They live in the same television-dominated, throwaway world as their "other side of the tracks" counterparts; and they face the same value vacuum. It is true that they own more things and do not face hunger, homelessness, or nearly as much violence. But their world has its share of drug abuse, crime, and parents who are there in theory but not in body or spirit. They are also latchkey kids who raise themselves while watching television and eating microwave food without parental interaction.

I was visiting an upper-middle-class high school in Mill Valley, California, when I overheard a teacher chastising a sophomore girl. The student gave her teacher a nasty look and said: "Don't tell me what to do. I make more in allowance than you do in salary. I don't have to listen to you. If you have a problem, take it up with my father . . . if you can find him." Children like this sophomore face significant, if different, risks than the poor child who has his shoes stolen for liquor money.

At least the ghetto child is aware of the present danger. The Mill Valley student might not even be aware that anything is wrong.

The social ills that are eroding our culture cannot be cured by school alone. In addition to education, a massive change in national priorities must occur. But that does not mean that schools cannot play an important role in making things better. As long as children remain hopeless, they are high risk not only in school but for life. Cynicism is self-defeating and destroys the will to survive and to flourish. Schools can, and must, reach the hopeless and inspire the will to succeed. Hopeful students become the leaders of tomorrow.

The more hopeful children become, the more educated they will become. With education come the skills for jobs, the understanding needed to raise healthy children of their own, and, most importantly, the skills to develop the quality of life that makes living worthwhile. Educated children will be less likely to become adults who are easily manipulated by the media and others who benefit from a less-educated populace. Education is the best chance our children have to live meaningful lives, to refuse to settle for just staying alive.

As long as we have hope that children can receive a worthwhile education, there will always be hope for our culture to find itself. Schools can encourage, model, and value caring about individuals. The school can be a place where differences in people are seen as positive and enriching, rather than as a source for strife. Maryleen Stettner, a first grade teacher in San Francisco, was teaching a unit on famous African-Americans during African-American awareness month when one of her African-American students asked her if he could study white people, too. When she asked Chris why, the whole class responded by saying, "He loves white people. He loves you and you're white." The more schools can do to nourish and support attitudes such as Chris's, the greater the chance of altering the anger that pervades the fabric of America. Maybe schools cannot change society by themselves, but I cannot think of a better place to start.

------

1. Frymier, Jack, and Gansneder, Bruce, "The Phi Delta Kappa Study of Students at Risk," *Phi Delta Kappan* 71, 2 (1989): 142.

2. Peterson, Karen, "When Old Spouses Haunt New Marriages," *USA Today*, 11 April 1991, p. 4D.

3. Smolowe, Jill, "To Grandma's House We Go," *Time Magazine*, 5 November 1990, p. 86.

4. Berman, Claire, *Adult Children Of Divorce Speak Out* (New York: Simon and Schuster, 1991).

5. Toufexis, Anastasia, "Struggling for Sanity," *Time Magazine*, 18 October 1990, p. 47.

6. Minow, Newton, "Television Today: More Choice, But Where's The Vision?" *USA Today*, 10 May 1991, p. 12A.

7. Howard, Lucy, and Cerio, Gregory, "Millions of Kids Go Hungry," *Newsweek*.

8. Morganthau, Tom, and Cohn, Bob, "America's Arsenal," *Newsweek*, 8 April 1991, p. 31.

9. "Young Men in Jeopardy," *USA Today*, 11 April 1991, p. 13A.

10. Mead, Walter Russell, "The New Old Capitalism: Long Hours, Low Wages," *Rolling Stone*, 30 May 1991, p. 27.

11. Strong, Larry, "The Best Kids They Have," *Educational Leadership* (February 1989): 2.

Three

Hope, Risk, and Learning

"There's no time to lose," I heard her say.
"Cash your dreams before they slip away.
Dying all the time.
Lose your dreams and you will lose your mind."

— "Ruby Tuesday"
The Rolling Stones

HOPE IS AMONG THE MOST POWERFUL of human feelings. It inspires and is inspired by the most significant events of our lives. We need hope to fall in love; falling in love makes us hopeful. Hope is intimately related to the birth of our children, graduating from high school and college, getting a job. Even going to war requires and inspires hope for a better world. We love, marry, divorce, kill, procreate, and live through our visions of hope.

When hope is lost, so is the reason to try. Without hope, we can still love, kill, procreate and live, but we do so in a vacuum. We function on automatic pilot, without inspiration and without zeal. When we feel most hopeless, life seems intolerable. Our energy is focused on protection and escape. Escape comes in many forms, from midlife rejections of our lifestyles, leading to what seem to be sudden changes in jobs and marriage partners, to vegetating in front of the television for many hours at a time. Drug addiction and suicide are extreme forms of escape.

Almost one quarter of all adolescent deaths are from suicide. Harkavy Friedman reports that 60% of samples of adolescents studied had suicidal thoughts and 9% of high school students studied reported having made a suicide attempt.[1] Barbara Barrett Hicks says that:

> *Suicide is not a bizarre and incomprehensible act of self destruction...Rather suicidal youth use a logic and a style of thinking which brings them to the conclusion that death is the only solution to the problems they are facing.*[2]

I believe that suicidal children have not only lost hope for finding less radical solutions to their problems, but are also hopeful that death will, at least, provide relief.

Perhaps the most common form of escape is to stop caring. When a child says, "I could care less," he means that to care more means to hurt, and he doesn't want to hurt any more.

Hope is multifaceted and hard to pin down. Sometimes hoping is like dreaming or wishing for something to happen that is beyond control—hoping for a special man or woman to call, or hoping to win the lottery, for example. Sometimes hoping involves taking action—hoping you will get the job you applied for, or hoping for that special person to accept your invitation. Sometimes hope means faith—knowing deep inside that things will turn out the way you want. Marlene Veach says, in a newspaper article describing her brother, Astronaut Lacy Veach:

*So what makes my brother one of the elite? What
makes Lacy exceptional, like the other astronauts
and everyone else who has ever achieved what
others consider unachievable? I believe that it's
the undeviating level of conviction and acceptance of a dream as not only possible and attain-
able, but already attained. I've seen my brother's
drive and desire. For as long as I can remember,
he has known that he would one day be strapped
in on the launch pad at Kennedy Space Center.[3]*

People with hope chase rainbows, and sometimes catch
them. Those without hope see little reason to try. They do not
believe that rainbows can be caught and that even if a rainbow
could be caught, it would be nothing more than colored mist.

Rollo May says about wishing (which I associate with
hoping):

*The human wish...is not merely a push from the
past, not merely a call from primitive needs
demanding satisfaction. It also has in it some
selectivity. It is a forming of the future, a mold-
ing by a symbolic process which includes both
memory and fantasy, of what we hope the future
will be. The wish is the beginning of orienting
ourselves to the future, an admission that we
want the future to be such and such; it is a
capacity to reach down deep into ourselves and
preoccupy ourselves with a longing to change the
future.[4]*

LEARNING AND RISK

My personal experience with hope has been that it was an
essential element for anything I have ever achieved. Hope pro-

vided the courage and the incentive to overcome seemingly impenetrable barriers. It also intensified the loss and feeling of pain when I was unsuccessful. Hope did not seem so wonderful during times of failure; and at those times, I told myself how foolish I was to be so naive and idealistic.

Hope and learning are inseparable for me. Everything I learned increased my hope that my life would be somehow enhanced, and that made me hopeful for new learning opportunities.

Learning requires taking risks because learning changes you. It challenges your perceptions and understanding of the way things are. It makes life more complicated. Learning provides not only new skills and tools but also the need to use them. For example, learning even a single new word gives you a new way to frame a thought.

Taking risks requires hope, which is a double-edged sword. It increases the chances for success and intensifies the pain of failure. When continued failure interferes with the ability to hope, learning will not occur. The loss of hope needs to be understood as lethal to intellectual and psychological development. Without a balanced set of successful experiences, it becomes *increasingly difficult to continue to take risks.*

High risk students are, in a sense, students who will not take risks. They will not risk doing what schools want them to do because they have little hope for success. Protection becomes more important than taking risks. When high risk students see other students being successful, they begin to doubt that they belong in school. As long as they believe that they do not belong in school, that school was created for the other students, they will tell us in every way possible that we can have their bodies but not their spirit. Their energy will be spent on protecting and escaping, not learning. If we want to reach them, then we must change their perception of school and increase their willingness to risk being hopeful.

CREATING A CLIMATE FOR RISK AND HOPE

Students at risk come to school with little hope that they will be welcomed by teachers, administrators, and other students. They have little hope of being successful in the academic tasks they will be asked to do. They wake up every morning expecting to be told, in one way or another, that they are stupid, slow, useless, arrogant, lazy, and in trouble. They face 180 of these mornings if they go to school every day. If they have one or two good days, their expectations will not change a great deal. Their expectations will not change until that exceptional good day becomes routine.

Imagine how different learning would be for these students if when they woke up in the morning, they were excited about going to school; if on the way to school, they thought about how happy their arrival would make everyone they saw and how well they would do in their subjects that day; if they knew that their teacher would call on them and say, "Great job," when they finished their task. When they opened the door and walked in, they would feel at ease, as if they belonged.

Until we address the expectations of students and provide them with a feeling of hopefulness, all the specific strategies to help them learn will exist in a context of defeat. Having higher expectations for them is important, but without providing the means for meeting those expectations, we will only increase the hopelessness of those students. William Firestone, who studied two similar high schools, one with more positive results with high risk students than the other, says:

*...an exclusive emphasis on order and high
expectations is a hard line position: it raises standards without providing help to meet them and
without necessarily increasing incentives. To alle-
viate alienation, the emphasis on order and
expectations must be accompanied by equal parts
of respect and relevance for students and professionalism for teachers.[5]*

To encourage students to risk learning, we need to alter
more than just our expectations of them. Comprehensive, integrated changes are required in the way we teach, the way we
discipline, and the way we relate to these students in both
social and personal situations. If we limit our efforts to adding
occasional programs, we will limit the change in student perception to having a few good days in a generally hostile environment.

There are two conditions we must create in order to
encourage students to become actively involved in the learning
process. Maslow says the way to increase motivation is to
simultaneously decrease the dangers and to enhance the attractions.[6] If they are to get involved in the learning process, students who are reluctant to risk need something to hope for,
something to be gained to make the risk worthwhile. They
must overcome past failures and an attitude that predicts failure in the future (decreasing the danger). Learning activities
can succeed when they promise students competence in doing
what is important to them.

Traditional attractions, like going to college or getting
good grades, are often not the best motivators because they are
not goals to which these students currently aspire. Attractions
like these might actually have a detrimental effect, because
they have associations of failure for high risk students who

believe those goals are "for the other kids." These goals do not have to be permanently abandoned; they can be introduced later if the student, through smaller successes, increases his interest in school-oriented goals.

One attraction that does work for high risk students is to show them how the subjects taught in school will directly benefit them. Firestone says that when standards are raised, an accompanying need for relevance must be raised as well:

> *Students need a personal reason to meet standards. This need was less acute [in his study] with higher achieving students, but those having the greatest trouble in school took the narrowest view of what was worth learning:*
>
> *"I don't see the purpose of algebra. All you need is English and math. The rest just fills time."*
>
> *"In English you need to learn to speak and read right, but reading stories is pointless."*
>
> *The clearest way to show high risk students the relevance of schoolwork was to provide a short-term direct connection to future employability....Two factors contributed to students' perceptions that schooling was relevant. The first was the availability of career oriented programs in such areas as business, finance, technology, and Jr. ROTC...The second relevance factor was counseling.[7]*

The second condition involves students predicting a positive outcome from doing a learning activity. Students must feel that they can be successful in the endeavor. Despite how useful or attractive the goal is, without at least some belief that success is possible, students will be reluctant to add another failure to their list. To paraphrase Maslow, the greater the attraction, the greater the risk of danger. The more they want success, the more painful it becomes not to get it and the more the failure hurts.

Therefore, if the student is willing to risk trying, our responsibility is to establish optimal conditions for success. This includes designing curricula for the unique way each student learns best. We must encourage and support intellectual development of many kinds of thinking. There is more to the intellect than digesting and regurgitating information. Equal opportunities for creativity and artistic expression need to be developed.

The traditional school curriculum either ignores or underuses the abilities of many students who fail at typical analytical activities. Albert Einstein was a special education student in math when he was in seventh grade, largely because he was misunderstood. If students fail in activities that require a specific learning style, we need to find activities that use learning styles that maximize the way they learn. When we evaluate student learning, we must use grading systems that encourage learning and provide feedback to improve performance. Lists of how poorly students are doing will not inspire hope or encourage taking risks. Such lists do not help high risk students overcome the belief that school is not for them.

We need to understand and accept that a classroom is a collection of individuals, not merely a group. In short, we must shape the hole (the school) to fit all the pegs (the students).

Individualizing the curriculum will go a long way toward reclaiming the high risk student. However, more is necessary. We must also welcome high risk students as human beings. They come to school as whole people, not simply as brains waiting to be trained. Our assumptions about their social behavior need to include the understanding that their negative behaviors are based on protection and escape. They do the best they can with the skills they have under the adverse conditions they face. Their negative behavior is not always intended to be malicious. When they are malicious, they believe, rightly or wrongly, that they are justified in defending themselves from attacks on their dignity. The same factors that limit their academic performance also affect their social skills. We must provide them with the opportunities to learn social skills with the same understanding, compassion, and zeal as we do with academic skills. We must individualize and personalize solutions to problems of behavior. Once again, we must shape the hole to fit the peg.

In short, for students who are alienated, are fearful, or believe that school offers them nothing of importance, we must alter conditions to create hope. *Hope is the powerful antidote that can entice students into learning, and develop the commitment necessary to stay with it when learning becomes tough.* Encouraging hope involves increasing motivation to learn and simultaneously increasing successful learning opportunities. This book was written with the hope that schools can find a way to light students' internal fires, to make them welcome as people, to make them wake up hungry for the day's learning.

---

1. Hicks, Barbara Barrett, *Youth Suicide* (Bloomington, IN: National Educational Service, 1990), p. 13.

2. Ibid.

3. Veach, Marlene, "My Big Brother, Astronaut," *The San Francisco Chronicle*, 23 April 1991, p. B3.

4. May, Rollo, *Love and Will* (New York: Norton Press, 1969), p. 211.

5. Firestone, William, "Beyond Order and Expectations in High Schools Serving At-Risk Youth," *Educational Leadership*, (February 1989): 41-42.

6. Maslow, Abraham, *Toward a Psychology of Being* (Princeton, N.J.: D. Van Nostrand, 1962), p. 47.

7. Firestone, Op. Cit., p. 43.

Four

Professionalism and Hope

Don't refuse to go on an occasional wild goose chase; that is what wild geese are made for.

— Henry S. Haskins

DURING A PARTICULARLY LONG AND GRUELING series of inservice training sessions that crisscrossed the United States, I wound up in Carmel, Indiana. I was tired and worn out. Thirty minutes before I was scheduled to address the audience of about 150 educators, I gave myself permission to "get through the day" as best I could. I told myself that I would do my best under the circumstances and that would just have to be good enough.

An older woman interrupted my private excuse-making and extended her hand to me. As I shook her hand, she said, "I'm so glad to be here. I came all the way from Chicago to hear you speak, because my daughter heard you once and said that I had to hear you at least once in my life. This is the only inservice my school will allow me to attend this year, and I am so happy that it will be with you."

At that moment, I felt fairly stupid and unimpressed with my earlier decision to "just get by." This woman inspired me. Her statement confronted me with the reason I was there. It was not just to give a talk on "Discipline With Dignity." It was to give those teachers the skills for working with their students. It might have been my fourth presentation in a row, but it was their first and only opportunity with me.

For the entire two days of the workshop, I focused on the teacher who greeted me. I found energy I did not know I had. This experience helped me understand how powerful and renewing it is to focus on my purpose for being there. *No strategy or technique can replace the power of a sense of purpose.* Sometimes that sense of purpose gets lost or buried under other more immediate concerns. I was lucky that someone reached out to me and reminded me why I was there.

Hopeful attitudes by students begin with hopeful teachers and administrators. Before students can learn to be hopeful, they must interact with hopeful professionals on a daily basis. However, when teachers are tired of teaching and administrators are tired of administering, they are transformed from professionals into laborers who serve their time and do little else. Cynicism is the greatest danger to education; it is a potent, contagious disease that eats away at the energy and enthusiasm of all educators. There are many reasons why educators might legitimately feel cynical. Often, front-line educators, teachers, and building administrators face major responsibilities and lofty goals without the necessary resources, decision making power, or support. Many of the children in their schools do not want to learn or behave. The ills of society spill into the school where everybody expects they will be cured. The task is overwhelming. If educators are not clear about why they are working in schools in the first place, they are candidates for chronic cynicism. Many teachers bail out early; one-half of all new teachers quit after their first year.

Educators are true professionals. They need at least as much training, put in at least as many hours, and must keep up with at least as much information as all other professionals, including doctors, lawyers, judges, scientists, or CEO's. Yet teachers do not receive the same professional rewards. Educators do not earn the same amount of money that other professionals earn.

Educators do not attain the same levels of power. They do not take two-hour power lunches over martinis to make key decisions about the future of their work. They have little say in who their clients are, what their hours will be, where they perform, how they will be evaluated, or what classes they will teach. A single parent complaint can create a major change in the way they carry on their daily business. Politicians with no knowledge or understanding of education can do more harm in one minute than the good work of educators over years. A power lunch for a teacher is eating a bologna sandwich while running down the hall, trying to get to class before the students.

Educators do not have vast amounts of free time. Contrary to popular belief, teachers and principals do not end their day at 3:35. Evaluating student work and developing new activities keeps teachers up late at night. Administrators have meetings three to four nights a week, some ending after 10:00 p.m. The time educators spend, when they do their jobs well, is as much, if not more, than all other professionals.

American educators are not accorded a high level of prestige. In Asia and Europe, teachers are treated with the highest respect and honor. One time when I was in Europe at a reception, I was asked what I did. When I said I was a teacher, people fought over me, wanting me to sit at their table for the luncheon. I was presented with wine and baskets of fruit. "You're a teacher. Please, sit here. Accept this gift. I am honored to have you here." Asians and Europeans treat teachers almost as well as Americans treat football players. We say to athletes, "Please sit at my table. Here, have this car."

However, when educators tell Americans what they do, they are usually asked, "Why do you do that?" A teacher at a workshop I conducted in Seattle told the group, "I have a great answer when people ask what I do. I say I deal in futures. When they show interest, I say I have over two hundred clients a day. When they raise their eyebrows, I say with a sly smile that I take stock every single day."

I do not point all this out to depress anyone. There is no need for educators to begin writing letters of application for other jobs. When one becomes an educator for the right reason and is able to focus on that reason, cynicism fades into the background and the joy of teaching emerges to the forefront. *That reason is to make a difference in the lives of children.* Helping children is a wonderful, fulfilling profession that gives far more than it takes. Money never makes people happy in the long run. The lack of it does, without question, make people unhappy. But the addition of it will not make anyone a great deal happier. The recent history of lottery winners show that several either have blown all their money or wish they had never won. Money, like power, satiates. More is needed to maintain the same level of happiness. Think of how long it takes, after buying a new car, home, refrigerator, or stereo, to begin wishing for a better model. Look at professional athletes, like Rickey Henderson or Dwight Gooden, who say they are insulted by offers of only four million dollars a year and whine for more. Four million dollars a year would buy a lot of happiness if happiness could be bought. Helping children satisfies longer and more profoundly than the power and money acquired by working in more lucrative professions.

Parade Magazine published an article, "Is Teaching For You?", that examined some of the reasons why people become teachers.

By the time he was 30, Chuck Longfield had achieved the American dream. A former scholarship student at Harvard, Longfield had joined a start-up computer company after graduation and helped build it into a multi-million-dollar business. He'd become a partner and enjoyed a stimulating professional life. He had money and success. Yet he gave it all up.

"I wanted to do something really worthwhile with my life—something that mattered," says Longfield, now 34. "I'd once taught college classes at night and liked it. I felt I could make a difference teaching kids."

A decade ago, when teaching ranked among the least attractive professions in the U.S., stories like these would have been rare. But today, many Americans who decide to change careers—or start new ones in retirement—want to teach. They say that the intrinsic values of teaching, if not the financial rewards, are worth it.[1]

Every day when they wake up and go to work, teachers and administrators must remember why they are doing it: *to make a difference in the lives of children.* When the daily grind of school begins to erode their idealism and energy, they must reconnect with their most important and immediate reasons for being there. This is the first step in creating a hopeful environment for students.

When taught by teachers who have lost their sense of purpose, students feel more processed than educated. William

Firestone, reporting on a study of alienation in schools, explained:

> *Because teachers and students share the school environment and because each group is dependent upon the other to meet its needs and achieve its successes, teacher alienation and student alienation feed each other....The rank order correlation between teacher alienation and student alienation was .92, indicating a high degree of association....*

> *These findings suggest that creating a high quality school climate, where productivity and satisfaction and a sense of community prevail, is not likely to result from fragmented efforts. When principals and teachers recognize that student and teacher alienation are mutually reinforcing, they can direct strategies for improvement toward both groups.[2]*

Teachers generally believe that the greatest causes leading to high risk students are due to factors outside of the school and that there is little they can do about them. In the Phi Delta Kappa Study of Students At Risk, "Asked whether they thought it was possible for teachers to help students cope with various out of school problems, more than 60% of the teachers said `no' with regard to such problems as family discord, family instability, crime, and alcohol abuse; 45% reported they could not help students cope with substance abuse. In more than 90% of the cases, teachers thought that parents or students, rather than teachers, should be most responsible for helping students cope with such problems."[3]

It is not easy to change cynical attitudes to hopeful ones. Raymond Wlodkowski has said that teaching is a "hidden harvest" profession. You rarely see the results of what you teach. The differences you make come much later. Therefore, teaching requires an act of faith. The obstacles to success are more obvious on a daily basis than the successes themselves. Usually, it is the high risk students whom administrators see the most often. Teachers spend disproportionately more time and energy on students who will not learn and will not behave properly than on those who do. They try various strategies suggested in training and education courses, in books and articles, and by teachers. Few of these strategies make an immediate difference, or any perceptible difference at all. Educators begin to wonder if anything they do will matter.

The Phi Delta Kappa study of high risk students uncovered some interesting observations regarding educators' lack of confidence in the techniques they use with high risk students:

> *Various data suggest that the professionals surveyed lacked skill with or without confidence about particular approaches to working with at-risk students. For example, 99% of the principals reported that they regularly notified parents when they worked with students who were at-risk; 68% said that doing so was effective. And 99% said that they regularly conferred with the parents of students who were at-risk; 74% said that such conferences were effective. Likewise, 82% said that they regularly referred at-risk students to psychologists; 61% reported that the practice was effective. And 86% said that they emphasized the basic skills; 70% said that such effort was effective. Almost three fourths (71%) of the principals said that they regularly retained students in grade, but only 26% thought that retention was effective.*[4]

Teachers reported a similar lack of confidence that their classroom techniques were working. The same phenomenon occurs with discipline techniques. Most teachers and principals say that detentions, suspensions, writing names on chalkboards, and lectures do not make much difference with the hard-to-control students. When I ask them why they continue to do these things, they usually reply that they do not know what else to do and they have to do something.

There can be no hope if educators have no confidence in the techniques they use. Educators must give up the notion that "It's better than nothing." In the long run, it might be better to put more energy and effort into only those methods that teachers and administrators believe will actually improve things. Not only will there be more success with the students, but less cynicism on the part of the faculty.

Perhaps one of the biggest barriers to teachers for feeling hopeful is the number of assumptions about what constitutes learning and what constitutes a school. Schools operate with a "one size fits all" mentality. Students are expected to learn a curriculum and to behave in a manner that is determined before they get there. The students who are least successful have trouble functioning in a "school-like" manner. Teachers who expect all students to conform to these pre-established norms are more likely to be cynical than teachers who can adjust their teaching to fit the student. Carlos Castaneda makes the following observation in *A Separate Reality*. Include in his concept of "forces" the forces that drive students to behave the way they do.

> *The average man, in ignorance, believes that*
> *those [life's] forces can be explained or changed;*
> *he really doesn't know how to do that, but he*
> *expects that the actions of mankind will explain*

them or change them sooner or later. The sorcer-
er [he uses this term to mean a wise man, not a
magician], on the other hand does not think of
explaining them or changing them; instead he
learns to use such forces by redirecting himself
and adapting to their direction. That's his trick.
There is very little to sorcery once you find out its
trick.[5]

Changing expectations of the way schools function and adapting them to genuinely serve students is both frightening and overwhelming. But change is the driving force of hope. Hope is the belief that desirable changes can and do occur. Nothing will improve for students without a strong belief in and a firm commitment to comprehensive changes in the way schools function.

When hope is a school value, it is very powerful indeed. I worked with an elementary school in Mt. Diablo, California, where the main obstacle to improving school discipline was a severely ingrained and widespread cynicism among the faculty and staff. After a series of meetings, a small group of teachers and a very brave and new principal put their cards on the table and aired their concerns. Ultimately, they realized that their biggest enemy was the attitude of hopelessness that pervaded the school. They developed a plan to combat this attitude. Each teacher agreed to personally counsel and encourage any teacher who displayed cynical attitudes. They put up Ghost Buster-style signs with *Cynicism* in the middle of the red circle. They monitored negative comments in the faculty room and reminded those who made them that it was not acceptable to spread cynicism publicly, that it was better to find a new way to look at the problems they were facing. They had parties with the expectation that all faculty would come and bring food, gifts, and the like, to create a spirit of teamwork. The goal of this group of teachers was not to dictate how the other faculty and staff should feel, but to turn around a pervasive, negative orientation. The mere fact that they believed that deeply ingrained attitudes could be changed was the beginning of hope for the school. The next year was not free of problems; but the teachers and, equally important, the students felt a renewed attitude that problems could be attacked. Things began to improve.

The now famous T.E.S.A. studies shows that teacher expectations translate into student achievement. Along with expectations, attitudes and values directly influence student achievement. Here are my suggestions for schools, individual teachers, and administrators to develop and maintain hopeful attitudes.

SCHOOLWIDE (FOR THE ADMINISTRATOR)

The principal sets the tone for the school and is the most influential person in how successful it will be. The principal is the point player for the success of its innovations and its morale. A hopeful school is one with a faculty that trusts its administration—trusts enough to take chances without worrying about condemnation for nonsuccess, and trusts enough for honest communication to occur. When faculty are listened to and when suggestions are acted on quickly, productivity, taking risks with new ideas, and caring about students also increase. The administrative staff sends a powerful message when they exemplify an attitude of hope. The following suggestions do not replace hopeful attitudes and supportive behavior. They are offered to help translate these attitudes into action.

1. Establish an informal school value system that frowns upon cynical attitudes. That does not mean having "thought police" monitor every statement or behavior that sounds cynical. Teachers need room to breathe and to let

off steam occasionally without harping from their supervisors. However, long-term hopeless attitudes and behaviors corrupt and destroy potential for growth. Serious displays of cynicism should not be welcomed.

When teachers are chronically cynical, the administrator can and should step in and discuss what is going on with that teacher. Coaching techniques often can be used successfully to help those teachers find more appropriate expressions of their doubts and fears.

There is a difference between cynicism and skepticism. Teachers do not need to be encouraged to try ideas and techniques that feel wrong to them, but they can be encouraged to solve problems and make improvements in their own style. When cynical teachers find a receptive administration that accepts them for who they are, the need for cynicism diminishes.

2. Develop support systems to maximize the potential for the success of new ideas. Success quickly stops negativity; but often innovations are not given a chance to succeed because of the context within which they are placed. Be sure to provide all the resources necessary for an innovation to work. Most techniques require time before they result in positive gains, and teachers need encouragement to keep going. Teachers also need to discuss possible negative side effects of new techniques and how to deal with them. Time can be set aside during faculty meetings to discuss how techniques can be improved. Time should also be given to hear success stories when new methods work well.

3. Teachers need to be treated with dignity. It makes no sense to encourage teachers to enhance the dignity of their students if their own dignity is not valued.

4. Informal appreciation of teachers by administrators and informal appreciation of administrators by teachers can go a long way toward maintaining positive attitudes. School spirit might be seen as a hokey remnant of the Fifties that has no place in the reality orientation of the Nineties, but school spirit is not a bad idea. Pride in a school by the faculty and staff can increase many positive feelings. Having special days that celebrate education and *esprit de corps* are fun. Creating fun T-shirts about the school that are worn by the faculty and staff not only make school a more fun place to be, but also a more desirable place to be. Attending to details like these might seem trivial, but such special care has a strong cumulative effect.

5. Provide inservice training opportunities both on site and at conferences or training centers. New skills inspire hope. New skills for teachers and administrators inspire energy for attacking old problems with zeal.

   The best training programs are inspirational. They lift the spirits of the participants with a vision of what school can be. Training without a spiritual element fulfills only half of its mission.

   However, training that is *only* inspirational is likewise incomplete. When educators are inspired without learning new skills to translate that inspiration into action, they become even more cynical. When the inspiration of the training wears off and the same old problems still exist, teachers rightly wonder what the training message had to do with reality. They feel hurt, betrayed, and unwilling to put faith in the next training experience that comes their way. They behave similarly to high risk students who are offered encouragement but are not given any additional skills.

Those who are in charge of professional training need to take the care to provide a balance between inspiration and workable methods. They should provide a variety of training sessions to meet the individual learning styles and special needs of each teacher. The same level of planning for success that we advocate for students is appropriate for the training of teachers.

6. Administrators can schedule regular talk sessions with small groups of teachers to hear their concerns. If it can be arranged, take three or four teachers out to lunch for an hour. It might not be a "power lunch," but it will give you a chance to check the pulse of the school. Over the course of the year, meet with the entire faculty and staff. Be sure to act on what you hear in as short a time as possible. If your efforts to act on what faculty and staff request are unsuccessful, then get back with people and give them legitimate reasons why you cannot make the changes they wanted. If possible, offer alternative modifications that might be helpful in meeting the same needs. For example, if teachers wanted to have the option to use corporal punishment, an administrator might provide training in the use of other, more effective discipline techniques.

7. Be aware of difficult times of the year for faculty: the week before grades are due, the day before parent conferences, the week after vacation, the February doldrums. Cut demands on faculty during these times and increase your support and visibility. Do something unexpected, like starting school with coffee and bagels in the faculty room as a special, unexpected treat. It is more important to show that you understand and that you care than it is to buy food. Be there to talk with the faculty, shake their hands, listen to what they have to say.

8. Set up an open office period with nothing else scheduled. Make that time available for individual or small groups of teachers who want to talk with you, no appointments necessary. At faculty meetings, summarize what teachers are telling you and what can be done to improve the school based on that information. Do not allow that time to fill up with other activities. If no one comes to see you, use the time to read.

9. Do not discount the stress related to teaching. When teachers are under the strain of stress, they will not function at their best. Legitimize methods of stress reduction and encourage teachers to use stress-reduction techniques. It might help to reduce demands and expectations for teachers who are experiencing difficulties. Be flexible enough to shield teachers from pressure at various times, knowing that they will achieve more when they have their stress under control.

   There is an ebb and flow to teaching, and each faculty member has his or her own rhythm. By responding to the individual rhythm of each teacher, you can set an example for teachers to accept the individual patterns of their students.

10. Set up a school-visitation program. Visiting other schools has two payoffs. When teachers see schools that have less to offer than their own, they become grateful to be where they are. They appreciate their own backyard a little more. When they visit schools that function better than theirs, they come back with new ideas and strategies to try. Provide a forum for teachers who visit other schools to share their feelings and increased knowledge with other faculty and staff.

Invite other teachers and administrators to visit your school. Give them the opportunity to share what they liked during their visit and to offer any suggestions for improvement. Set an example for the faculty and staff to be open and non-defensive with all suggestions and observations.

INDIVIDUALLY (FOR THE TEACHER)

The suggestions that follow are not meant to replace the sense of purpose so essential for hopeful teaching. They are suggested to give you a reminder for those times when you need a little extra help to maintain that sense of purpose.

1. Remember why you are in the profession. Find a method to continually remind yourself that you are there to positively affect the lives of students. Each day, find a way to celebrate something that happens in school that tells you that you have somehow reached a student. For example, tell your family one success story during dinner and encourage them to do the same. Make it a family tradition.

2. Pick a student who seems to be alienated from school and personally welcome him or her every day for a week by simply saying, "Hello, good to see you here today."

3. Pick a teacher who seems to be alienated from school and personally welcome him or her every day for a week. Tell the teacher about a small success you have had in class recently and elicit a small success from that teacher.

4. Plan to do a classroom activity that you love every class period. The activity can be for the entire length of the class or for five minutes. On the way to school that morning, think of how much fun it will be when you do that activity with your students.

5. Shut off the television and read a book or article. Reading expands your perceptions and horizons. New studies indicate that television leads to depression. The right book or article might give you a positive suggestion for your classroom or school. Reading matter does not have to be limited to education. Newspapers, novels, poetry, and science magazines are filled with ideas that inspire new things to do with children in classroom settings.

6. Every month or two, bring in outside speakers to talk with your class. Choose local community people who have been successful in their fields and have the ability to articulate what made them successful and how school contributed to their success.

7. Ask other teachers for teaching strategies that work for them. If there are 30 teachers in your school and each offers three suggestions, then you will have a list of 90 strategies. Pick a strategy every two weeks and give it a try.

8. When cynical feelings emerge, do not fight them. Use them to your advantage. Feelings of hopelessness have their roots in situations that are not controllable. If you feel free to examine situations like these, you may discover two important points of positive affirmation. First, you cannot control everything that happens to you, but you can control how you deal with what happens to you. "Shit happens, but you don't have to step in it." There are always a multitude of responses to all situations. If you can identify the situation that generates cynicism, you can also identify a response that gives you, minimally, a sense of control. As you are able to take control, you will feel more hopeful.

   Second, you can change your expectations to match your abilities within the situation. No one has the ability to control another's behavior. You cannot control whether Johnny learns his vocabulary words, but you can control the methods you use to teach them. By disowning what other people do and not feeling personally responsible for their actions, you can take more pride and satisfaction in what you do.

By using your cynical feelings to identify areas in which you can gain more control, you will learn that you do not have to be a victim of circumstances. And there is the wonderful side benefit of setting an example, especially for those high risk students, of how to be hopeful under difficult, negative conditions beyond their control.

9. Use stress-management skills. There are a variety of stress-management techniques available, and many are written specifically for teachers. They range from esoteric new wave enlightenment to basic meditation techniques to physical exercises like aerobics. Find an approach that fits with your style and values, then use it regularly. Stress reduction can translate into cynicism reduction when used on a regular basis.

10. Communicate. Tell your students how you feel. Tell your administrator what is going well with you and what is worrying you as a teacher. Both your students and administrators can interact with you in a more positive manner when you are genuine with them. No one expects you to be a Pollyanna all the time, just as no one wants to be in the presence of a terminal grump. By genuinely communicating your concerns, you will be seen more as a whole person and less as one-dimensional. Hope always flourishes when people are whole.

These techniques are designed to keep you in touch with the energy and enthusiasm that lives inside of you. They cannot generate excitement for teaching that does not exist. Do whatever is possible to find a sense of hope in what you are doing. If it is there, you can find it.

However, if you are continually cynical and unhappy as a teacher, the question must be raised about whether it is time to find a different profession. More is at stake than whether education is right for you. A larger question is whether you are right for the children you teach. It is not a failure to realize that you are working in a profession that does not fit your values, skills, and personal orientation.

If you decide, after some soul searching, that teaching is for you, then understand why you feel that way; making a difference in the lives of children will be near the top of the list. Keep it close to your heart and your mind whenever you enter the school.

If you are an administrator who works with cynical teachers, you cannot avoid the same question. If the faculty member is continually unhappy and is spreading a feeling of hopelessness to students, then it is time to help that teacher assess whether teaching is the best profession for him or her.

Hope is affirming, healthy, and energizing. Students cannot learn without it. Teachers and administrators cannot do their jobs without it. Students deserve to be surrounded by hopeful professionals. They have a right to be taught by professionals with vision. My hope is that eventually, we can create schools that value hopefulness over all things.

---

1. Isaacs, Florence, "Is Teaching For You?," *Parade Magazine*, 18 November 1991, p. 11.

2. Firestone, William, "Beyond Order and Expectations In High Schools Serving At-Risk Youth," *Educational Leadership* 46, 5 (1989): 41.

3. Frymier, Jack, and Gansneder, Bruce, "The Phi Delta Kappa Study Of Students At Risk," *Phi Delta Kappan* 71, 2 (1989): 145.

4. Ibid.

5. Castaneda, Carlos, *A Separate Reality* (New York: Pocket Books, 1971), p. 214.

Five

Responsibility and Effective Discipline Techniques

People must never be humiliated—that is the main thing.

— Anton Chekov

MR. ELLISON HAS A SERIOUS DISCIPLINE PROBLEM with his computer. It refuses to do what he wants. He has tried every method he knows to get the computer to change its behavior. He scolded and lectured it. He gave it a detention and put it in another room for an hour. He suspended it and wrote its name, IBM 386, on the blackboard. Still, the computer refused to do what he wanted. Finally, out of desperation, he gave it a hard right jab. Unfortunately, the computer behaved even worse.

Until Mr. Ellison finds the right key to use in the right way, no form of punishment will change the computer's behavior. Mr. Ellison must change the way he deals with the computer because the computer is programmed that way. The same can be said of children. Punishing them won't change them because they are programmed that way. The right key must be found and used in the right way in order to reach them.

I had an enlightening experience while visiting Casa Grande Middle School in Casa Grande, Arizona. Jodie Summerfield, the principal, invited me to the school and gave me a tour of the facilities. It was similar to many warm climate schools in Arizona, Texas, California, and New Mexico, in that the classrooms opened to an open courtyard. There were no inside corridors whatsoever. Students passed between classes on a concrete walkway around the courtyard.

Mr. Summerfield said, "When I first took over as principal, there were fights every time the students changed classes. The previous principal tried detentions, suspensions, and parent conferences to stop them, but nothing worked. I stopped the fighting in three weeks. Guess how I did it."

I guessed all the techniques from my repertoire, mostly from the *Discipline With Dignity* program, but he said no to all of them. When I finally gave up he said, "I widened the walkway by three feet. You know, middle school kids have a code of behavior which they never violate. If you bump, you fight. No exceptions. If you bump, you fight. Well, the walkway was too narrow, so they bumped and they fought. By widening the walkway, they stopped bumping and stopped fighting."

How obvious and simple his solution was. How often do we put high risk students in situations that make it impossible for them to do what we want, and then get angry with them when they break the rules. We put students in situations they cannot control, and then we get angry with them for doing what is natural.

Discipline With Dignity, co-authored by Allen Mendler and myself, describes in-depth a plan for discipline. In this chapter, I adapt key elements of that plan to relate specifically to high risk students. Reading *Discipline With Dignity* provides a comprehensive overview omitted from this chapter.

Discipline for high risk students is different than for most students because of five powerful influences:

1. Students at risk have accumulated long histories of academic failure. Because of their academic histories, traditional school-based incentives have little or no motivational impact on them. Very often, children feel that it is better to be bad than it is to be stupid. They have very little to lose by misbehaving and very little to gain by being good citizens. Low-achieving students protect their dignity by behaving as inappropriately as they possibly can.

   To see how this works, simply ask yourself, if you got a 56 on an important test, what would make you feel better about failing? Telling your friends, "I studied hard and was just too stupid to pass." Or, "It was a stupid test anyway, and besides I hate that dumb class and that boring teacher." As long as it feels better to misbehave than it does to follow rules, traditional methods of discipline are ineffective.

2. The dignity of students at risk has been attacked since their early years of school, and it is through misbehavior that they pay the school back. A self-fulfilling prophesy is created when the students are labeled "behavior or discipline problems." They soon learn that they can always be good at being bad, and being bad meets their needs for attention, for power (to make others respond to them), and for fitting into a clearly defined niche. They often find other students with similar difficulties and bond with

those students. Feeling part of a group gives them a sense of identity and makes it more difficult to change them.

3. One of the strongest motivations for breaking rules is to fight against a system that diminishes self-worth and importance. Adults fight against systems when systems are perceived as too big, too impersonal, too cold-hearted, and too interested in preserving their own needs rather than the needs of their clients. Examples are credit card or credit report companies that refuse to acknowledge their mistakes, the IRS when it ignores its own rules and demands more taxes and penalties, and insurance companies that cancel a long-standing customer who gets into an accident.

    Students in school respond in the same way when the school presents itself as an impersonal, cold, self-preserving system. Students at risk quickly deduce that they are not told to be good in order to benefit them, except in a very roundabout way. They are asked to behave for the good of the system, a system that has rejected them. They fight to protect themselves against a force that is much larger and stronger than they are.

4. Students who are labeled "discipline problems" are systematically removed from opportunities to behave responsibly. Students who fight on the playground are removed from the playground until their behavior improves. Children who fight are told how and when to make up with the students they fought. Students with poor time-management skills are told when to do their work and when they can play.

    While the above scenarios sound perfectly natural on the surface, further analysis reveals how self-destructive these policies are. No one would tell a batter who was struggling at the plate that he could not participate in batting practice until he improved. No one would tell a poor reader that he could not look at any books until his reading improved. In the same way, no student can learn how to play on a playground by being removed from the playground, or how to learn time-management skills by being told when to schedule everything. By removing children with poor social skills from social situations, their skills remain underdeveloped. Responsibility is not a spectator sport. Learning responsibility requires participation.

5. As students come to accept the label, "discipline problems," their misbehavior becomes normal. Their behavior isolates them from the other students in class. Not only are they unable to do the academic school work, but they also are bothersome and irritating. They are in the way, and everyone, except their cohorts, is glad when they are absent. No matter which way they turn, they receive a negative message. The hopelessness that comes from being labeled a discipline problem is even worse than that which comes from being labeled an academic failure. Now the child is "a bad person."

Effective discipline for all children, and especially for those students who are at risk, is based on the following principles:

Principle 1. Dealing with student behavior is part of the job.

Some teachers believe that their job is to teach content material rather than the whole student. They see discipline as an intrusion on their time and energy. They do not want to be mothers, nurses, psychiatrists, or baby-sitters. They are like therapists who say, "I love being a therapist, I just hate to hear peoples' problems." Being a professional means behaving in any role that helps the client.

A more helpful and professional belief is that discipline problems are opportunities to teach students responsibility. Teachers who consider discipline to be part of their job are less stressed by students who act up, and are able to take a professional stance with those students. I advocate having as much energy and enthusiasm for discipline as you do for content. In the long run, teaching will be far more rewarding for you and for your students.

Principle 2. Short-term solutions often become long-term disasters.

Americans worship speed. We think in short stories, not novels. Trained on the half-hour sitcom, Americans expect problems to be solved in twenty minutes and change. Managers of fast-food restaurants know that patrons must be served their meals within $3\frac{1}{2}$ minutes of the time they enter or business begins to drop. Meals are often eaten even faster. At home, meals are often eaten quickly so they do not interfere with a television show.

Even television news stories are shorter. The average length of a TV "sound bite" declined from 42.3 seconds in 1968 to 9.8 seconds in 1988.[1]

We deal with social problems with the same attention span. The results are often short-term solutions leading to long-term disasters. Examples throughout our society include: our energy policy, our national fiscal policies, the way we treat our precious natural resources.

Most discipline techniques used in school are short-term answers designed to allow the teacher to return to "teaching." Detentions, writing names on boards, shouting, scolding, public humiliation and sarcasm, and sending to the principal's office are long-term disasters.

Any discipline technique that stops misbehavior and simultaneously reduces the desire to learn is disastrous. For at risk students short-term solutions are especially dangerous because they attack an already wounded self-concept and reinforce the belief that they can succeed only if they fail.

When evaluating discipline interventions, it is not enough to simply stop the misbehavior. Discipline problems cannot be solved by methods that set the stage for more serious problems and academic failure at a later time.

Principle 3. Always treat students with dignity.

Although some critics claim that too much time can be spent on self-esteem in the classroom, the need for dignity can never be overrated. Dignity is a basic need, essential for life.

If you recall two teachers you had as a student, one with whom you still are angry and another teacher whom you still love, you will find that the only difference between the two is that the former attacked your dignity and the latter enhanced it. If you are like most people, you learned more from the teacher you loved. Dignity is not simply about warm fuzzies, it is about what works. When we treat students with dignity, we have a better chance of helping them learn about both behavior and academics. When we attack students' dignity, we might get them to follow rules, but we lose them as students and as lovers of learning. To see how dignity affects learning, simply compare the dignity of the high risk student with those students who are most successful. The difference is startling.

Students at risk, almost by definition, suffer from attacks on dignity. Further attacks on their dignity make them harder to reach. Discipline methods must enhance the dignity of these students and offer the hope that it is possible for them to behave in acceptable ways. Discipline methods and techniques must do more than solve the immediate problems; they must be long-term solutions that change the perceptions of the students, alter their labels, and develop pride.

Dignity is a useful screen, or determiner, of whether any given intervention will improve behavior in the long run. When selecting an intervention, ask yourself these questions: "How will this technique or strategy affect the student's dignity?" "How would this strategy affect my dignity if a teacher did it to me?"

Principle 4. Good discipline does not interfere with student motivation.

Discipline techniques that control behavior but reduce student motivation to learn cause more problems than they solve. The balance between discipline and motivation cannot be ignored. Motivated students cause fewer discipline problems and are easier to discipline when they do cause problems. Students learn more when motivated. But motivation is fragile. Great care must be taken to protect what motivation exists and to nurture it until it grows. Reducing motivation, even for supposedly good reasons, becomes a vicious downward cycle that ends in a crash.

High risk students need all the motivation they can get. Use motivation as a screen to determine how effective a discipline technique is. Ask yourself the question, "What happens to student motivation with this technique?" If motivation is reduced, eliminate the technique.

Principle 5. Responsibility is more important than obedience.

Obedience means "do as you are told." Responsibility means "make the best decision possible." The obedience/responsibility continuum is another screen with which to evaluate the overall effectiveness of a discipline technique. If immediate safety is not a factor, then eliminate any discipline technique that promotes obedience at the expense of responsibility.

Responsible behavior and obedient behavior are often the same. The behavior is the same whether one wears a seatbelt because the law says one has to wear it or because it might save one's life; in both instances a seatbelt is worn. The difference between responsible and obedient behavior is choice. Responsibility requires choice. Teaching children to be responsible requires giving children choices.

Because responsibility is determined by motivation and not by behavior, it is difficult to define and hard to recognize even when we see it. If you made a list of examples of responsibility throughout history, the majority of those on your list would have been labeled "behavior problems" by many of their contemporaries. George Washington, Joan of Arc, Mother Theresa, Gandhi, Albert Einstein, Galileo, John Lennon, and Martin Luther King, Jr. are all examples of "disobedient" responsible people. There are students who are considered to be behavior problems but who are behaving responsibly, even though they are not doing what the school wants. Only through communication and understanding can one tell whether students are misbehaving because they are immaturely seeking attention, or because they have no acceptable outlet to meet their basic needs.

There are times when obedience is preferable to responsibility. When health or safety is involved or when speed is essential, obedience is a more appropriate goal. When a student is smashing other students with a baseball bat, it makes no sense to ask how he feels about what he is doing or how he plans to change. The first order of business is to stop what he is doing; work toward a more responsible decision later. Obedience works faster than responsibility and is helpful when speed is required. However, obedience is a short-term solution; it can not sustain appropriate behavior over time. At some point, the student needs to behave responsibly.

There are dangers in using techniques that promote obedience at the expense of responsibility. Obedient children will listen to friends, television, or any other potentially unwise voice if it speaks with authority. As children grow older, there are more voices telling them what to do, and some voices are dangerous. Children need to learn how to make reasoned decisions based on thoughtful understanding of both the facts and, equally importantly, the process of making decisions. When looked at from this perspective, being obedient is a disability.

Furthermore, obedience is effective only when an authority is present. Many children who have not been taught to behave responsibly follow rules only when they are being monitored. When no authority figure is visible, they misbehave more frequently than other children. They have learned that they can do what they want as long as they do not get caught.

The danger of this attitude cannot be underestimated. It erodes our society in the most perverse ways. The savings and loan scandal was made by people who believed they could do what they wanted as long as they did not get caught. College sports are plagued with abuses by coaches and athletes who believe they can do what they want as long as they do not get caught. Productivity in business and industry is affected by people who have a "don't get caught" mentality. A potent example is that of the police, the bastion of obedience in our country. The Rodney King videotape graphically demonstrated that even some law enforcement officers will do what they want as long as they do not get caught.

Responsible people, unlike obedient people, do the right thing because it is the right thing to do. They take pride in needing no rewards for behaving appropriately, like the busboy in San Francisco who returned a bag of money containing approximately $300,000. When Mayor Art Agnos named a day in the busboy's honor, he was grateful but embarrassed at the attention. "It wasn't my money," he said, "why would I keep it?" The sad part about this story is that it was newsworthy enough for the mayor to make a big deal out of it. If it was the norm, if everybody would have done the same thing, no day would have been celebrated, but honesty would certainly be more widespread. Responsible children have been taught to make moral or higher-level decisions. They tend to make decisions based on what is good rather than on what will avoid punishment.

The majority of at risk students come to school lacking the skills to behave responsibly. There are many reasons for this, including the reduction of time during which students interact with their parents and the increase in the amount of time they watch television. Schools do not help high risk students to gain these skills when they remove difficult students from situations requiring responsible behavior.

Children who do not learn how to behave responsibly at home either learn at school or run a risk of not learning at all. There are other places where children might learn responsible behavior—sports, religious activities, youth groups, and even "on the street"—but none of these activities has the potential to reach all children the way that home or school does.

Responsibility is too important to leave to chance, both for our society at large and for the individual student who will eventually need the skills of responsible behavior to survive as an adult.

Anger is the most difficult feeling to express in an acceptable manner at school and one of the most difficult to control. All students, and especially those who receive the most negative messages from school, should be provided outlets to express their feelings of anger and taught how to express those feelings responsibly. Students should also be taught how to tell teachers or administrators what they need, so they won't use rule breaking to express themselves. When students do express their feelings or communicate their needs, they should be heard.

Teaching students to behave responsibly requires 1) providing them opportunities to practice and 2) trusting that they will improve at making correct decisions. Poor choices lead to improved responsibility if students learn from them. View a student's poor choice as an opportunity to learn.

In addition to needing opportunities, students need the following subskills, which lead to responsible behavior.

- Awareness

- Predictability

- Real choices

- Planning

These skills can be taught as part of the curriculum. Once these skills have been learned, they are easier to introduce as part of a comprehensive plan for improving student behavior. Using the same skills both for behavior management and for teaching critical thinking conveys a very powerful message to students.

---

1. Alter, Jonathan, "Voters to Press: Move Over," *Newsweek*, 14 October 1991, p. 29.

Six

Diagnosing the Problem

U NDERSTANDING THE REASON WHY a student breaks a rule is essential to finding the best solution to the problem. Sally, the teacher of a fourth-grade special education class of inner city youth, had one student who came from a sexually and physically abusive home. Sally is an excellent, dedicated teacher who cared for this student both professionally and personally. She tried very hard to reach and connect with this student in a positive way. Eventually, Sally became the one person the student cared for and trusted.

The student began stealing from Sally—things from her desk, money, and even things from her pocketbook. Sally was so upset with this flagrant betrayal that she was ready to give up and write the girl off, once and for all. I suggested that maybe the girl was stealing because she wanted to take a piece of the teacher home with her, to keep Sally with her symbolically at all times. Sally tried giving the student as a present a belt that the girl had admired many times. The stealing stopped. Eventually the girl had to be institutionalized because her emotional problems were so severe, and when Sally visited her, she was still wearing the belt, many months later. The staff said she rarely took it off. In this case, it was strong love, not betrayal, that motivated the stealing, and if only the behavior was considered without understanding the motivation, all the parties involved could have been sadly hurt. The student is now doing well at a foster home.

Students often break rules because they do not have any other way to meet basic needs or because they do not know any other way to meet those needs. If you can identify what the student is asking for (in some cases, screaming for), you can provide experiences that will make life significantly better for both of you. Behaviorists believe that the motivation behind misbehavior is irrelevant, and the only significant, measurable variable is what the student does. However true this view might be in clinical situations, it is confounded in actual classrooms because of the complexity of an environment that consists of multiple reinforcers, interpersonal connections between students, social and home influences which affect classroom behavior, and students whose basic physiological and psychological needs are going largely unmet.

It is even more important to understand why students at risk break rules, because most of the traditional methods of discipline have not worked with them. Continuing ineffective methods will produce the same dismal results. It makes more sense to try techniques specifically designed for these students. These techniques will be most successful if they are based on the reasons why the rules are being broken.

Occasionally asking the students why they misbehaved will produce helpful answers. More often than not, one of the following two answers will be given:

"I don't know."

"He did it first."

A more reliable method of diagnosis is to observe the student in action, to talk with the student about many things, to ask gentle yet probing questions, and to do some sleuthing like an old-fashioned detective. Hypotheses must be checked. Sometimes, suggesting a hypothesis to the student might provide insight. Testing hypotheses is usually more productive than simply asking the student why he did it.

"Johnny, it seems to me that you are bored a lot of the time. My guess is that one of the reasons you are out of your seat all the time is that you are trying to entertain yourself."

"Diane, I think you wish you got more attention in this class. Do you want more attention?"

"Lyn, my guess is that the reason you are always speaking while I am talking is because you think it is stupid for you to sit quietly when you have something to say."

Once you have an idea of why students break rules, it becomes possible to experiment with creating conditions which allow students to meet their needs in an acceptable manner. The most common reasons why rules are broken by students at risk are related to the factors discussed earlier: dignity, power, escape behavior, and attack behavior.

There are more immediate reasons that are easier to treat if you understand them. To help understand what your students experience when they break rules, try to recall a time in your life when you broke a rule. Relive the experience as fully as possible in your imagination, recalling the fun, the danger, the way it affected your dignity and feelings of power, and whether it was worth it to you to misbehave even if you got caught. Identifying with children in similar situations will go a long way in helping you find avenues to reach your students.

Below are some common reasons for breaking rules and some suggestions for preventing them.

1. *It is fun and exciting.* Students who are not actively involved spend a great deal of time being bored. Breaking rules is one way to increase stimulation and reduce boredom. The risk of getting caught often adds to the fun; and for those that are often caught, it rarely serves as a deterrent.

Suggestions: Provide fun, positive activities and encourage the at risk children to participate. Use learning games, role playing, debating, simulations, and other activities that encourage laughter, creativity, playfulness, and hamming it up. Give leadership roles to the children who are in need of more fun-filled activities.

2. *It is easier.* Breaking rules is often a short cut to reaching a goal or fulfilling a demand. People speed on the highway because it is easier than being late. Students cheat on assignments because it is easier than doing them. People lie because it is easier than telling the truth.

Suggestions: Misbehaving often looks easier, but in the long run it is not. When students are taking shortcuts, make sure they know a different, more efficient manner to do things the right way. Make sure they understand the directions and have alternative methods for reaching the goal.

3. *The rules are stupid.* One of the most commonly mentioned reasons why people break rules is that they are perceived as stupid. Stupid rules are followed only when the odds of getting caught are great. Examples of stupid rules abound in school settings, such as silently lining up before going to lunch or bans on Bart Simpson T-shirts. Stupid rules not only are broken more often than sensible rules, but they also generate a disrespect for those who make and enforce them.

Suggestions: Review all rules that are broken frequently. Ask yourself if you would consider them stupid if you were the age of the students in your school or class. Ask your students what rules they think are the most stupid or the most meaningless to them.

If you honestly believe that the rule is stupid, change it. If you need administrator support, make a solid case for eliminating the rule. It helps to have an alternative, more sensible rule to offer as a substitute.

If you believe the rule is not stupid, explain to your students the reasons for the rule. If the rule is based on a principle that makes sense to the students, there is a good chance they will accept the rule.

There will be many instances when you might believe a rule is sensible and your students do not. It is worth taking the time to discuss the differences of opinion with your students and to hear what they have to say about it. Maybe you can find alternative rules that make sense to your students.

One other strategy is to discuss with the class as a whole, and with certain students individually, what the best methods are to deal with stupid rules. Talk about how you deal with them in your life and ask students how they deal with them. Just admitting the rules are stupid and being open to discuss them may go a long way toward encouraging students to follow them.

4. *To counterattack.* Students break rules when they feel their dignity has been attacked and they feel a need to counterattack. Sometimes the counterattack comes directly in the form of aggression. Students swearing at the teacher, being surly, or getting into a public power struggle are examples. Sometimes, the attacks are passive aggressive, involving withdrawal, silence, or such sneaky annoyances as tapping pencils,

coming in late, handing in messy work, or knocking something off another's desk.

Suggestions: The most important method of minimizing student counterattacks is to eliminate the attacks that triggered them. Take care when disciplining students, giving feedback for work, and in personal interactions. Maintain respect for the students' dignity at all times. Make this a high priority.

Sometimes a student will feel that his dignity has been attacked although the teacher does not think he has behaved in an attacking manner. Dignity is perceptual, and whether or not you think you meant to hurt someone's feelings, it is best to talk with the student about it when you see counterattacking behavior.

If the student is counterattacking, then a private discussion is in order. It helps to apologize and to tell the student that you understand how it feels to have your dignity attacked. Differentiate between feeling sorry about hurt feelings and allowing misbehavior to continue. Make sure you personally greet the student each day in a friendly manner, and show an active interest in the student for a significant period of time.

5. *To gain respect and to get the attention of peers.* Even if the audience, the other students, disapprove of public classroom misbehavior, they are entertained by it; and the reputation of the actors is enhanced. Any publicity, good or bad, helps a student get noticed. The game of chicken is played to win the respect of peers; the first to pull out of the way is the loser. In school, children play chicken by misbehaving. The winners are those who get the closest to the edge of danger.

The goal is to get noticed and respected for outlandishness, not sense. While increasing the penalty discourages many players, it increases the stakes for others. High risk students have very little to lose; they have a great deal to gain.

Suggestions: Lower the stakes. Reduce the penalties for behavior you can accurately classify as playing chicken. When you interact with a student who is showing off, do it privately, no matter how much the student tries to pull you into the public arena. When you must respond in front of the other students, do so with humor and diffusion strategies.

Student: *"You smell."*

Teacher: *"Thanks for caring enough to notice. You are the only one in class who bothered to point it out."*

Or:

Student: *"This class really sucks!"*

Teacher: *"You must be very angry to say that to me in front of the entire class. Let's talk about this later when we can be alone."*

Diffusion strategies take the sting out of the confrontation and often elicit laughter. You have now won the game of chicken, but the student has not lost: a win-win situation.

Equally important is to find as many ways as possible to give the student a chance to impress the other students in positive ways. Teach the student other ways to get attention without needing to play chicken.

6. *To maintain psychological distance from the school.* Students who want to escape from school but cannot do it physically can do it psychologically. By breaking rules and misbehaving, students can disassociate themselves from the school. When the student must stay in school and does not want to, there is a good chance that this reason is part of the motivation to misbehave.

Suggestions: This problem is caused by hopelessness and alienation. Remove the reasons for students to want to distance themselves from school. Find ways to make school more pleasant. Welcome them every day. Diminish the causes of alienation and helplessness that these students experience on a daily basis.

7. *To force the school to give up on them.* When students face failure every day, they often find peace in accepting failure once and for all. By accepting failure, they no longer have to worry about whether they will be successful. They feel similarly to someone who has been trying to give up smoking off and on for years with no permanent results, who eventually accepts the label, "smoker." Now they can smoke without guilt.

Suggestions: In the movie *The Terminator,* a cyborg is sent from the future to assassinate a woman. He is relentless in his quest. Even after he is blown up, the cyborg's metal skeleton still stalks its target. When the skeleton is crushed, the hand continues the quest. If the movie had continued longer, the fingernail would have relentlessly continued the attack. Like the Terminator, teachers must be relentless in letting students know that they will not give up on them, even if the students try to fail. Teachers should not embarrass, ridicule, or humiliate students for trying to fail. More important is that teachers must constantly promote the message, "I will never give up on you, so stop trying to make me."

Seven

Discipline Methods that Do Not Work

I ONCE VISITED THE WESTERN CANADIAN PRAIRIE known as the Pallicer Triangle. After a rather long ride through the plains, we came upon a small herd of antelope. They moved swiftly and effortlessly across the land until they encountered a wire fence. Without missing a step, they gracefully rolled down and under the fence and, once on the other side, jumped up and resumed their journey.

I thought of the number of children in school who in their own way jaunt gracefully throughout their lives. When the school puts up a fence trying to restrict their behavior, they roll down and under the fence and continue on their way. The following are some typical fences that schools put up to stop students and why it is so easy for students to slip under them.

1. *Scolding and lecturing.* Telling students what they have done wrong and what they should be doing has little effect on those who continually break rules. They know everything you can tell them before you say it, because they have heard it all before. By telling them what they should be doing, you reinforce in them that you believe they are incapable and stupid.

2. Sending to the principal (or assistant principal) for fixing. In the old television show, *Father Knows Best,* Bud would harass his sister, Kathy, who would then complain to her mother. Margaret would then tell Bud, "You wait till your father comes home." The reason she said this was that "father knew best." If mother knew best, she would have handled it. Everyone in the family, including Margaret, learned that mother was a wimp and father was in control.

When teachers send students to the principal, every student in class learns that the teacher is a wimp, that the teacher cannot handle the child without help. In addition, sending a high risk student to the principal further increases the distance between the teacher and the student. After the student has been sent to the principal, there is little the principal can do without the teacher present. The principal should be brought in only when the rule violations are serious, such as when a law has been broken.

3. Sarcasm. Teasing is a form of affection, unlike its dark cousin, sarcasm—which is a form of control. Being sarcastic with students might make us seem like "one of the boys," with them because they will laugh and tease back. But if you cross the line and attack their dignity, they might never forgive you, especially if you do it in public. Using sarcasm as a discipline technique leads to power struggles and eventually to humiliation and counterattacks. High risk students do not need further humiliation and power struggles in school. Using sarcasm with the high risk student is like throwing gasoline on a fire.

4. Writing name on the chalkboard. Like sarcasm, writing names on chalkboards attacks the dignity of the child and uses humiliation to force him or her into behaving. For students who need attention, writing their name is like putting it in lights on a marquee; it will encourage more negative behavior.

For students who feel unwelcome in school, writing their names on the board will destroy any potential link between them and the school. It is a way to write them off, to subdue them until they disappear.

5. *Corporal punishment.* Corporal punishment is harmful to students for three reasons. The first is that corporal punishment might lead to suicide. Psychologists linked corporal punishment with increased aggression, vandalism, and delinquency and have suggested links with depression and lowered self-esteem.[1]

The second reason is that spanking is used selectively. Corporal punishment is administered to minorities and disabled kids twice as often as to other students.[2] I have not seen statistics on the number of high risk students who are spanked, compared to other students, but I can guess. So can you.

The third reason is that schools do not allow students to hit each other. What kind of example is set when administrators or teachers hit students? Because students watch what we do so carefully, it is impossible to teach them to solve their problems by talking when we solve our problems by hitting.

There are simply not enough role models for children to see who do not use force to solve problems. Television, movies, radio, comic books, cartoons, and far too many parents blow the opposition away in one form or another. Schools must do more than give lip service to problem-solving techniques; schools also must demonstrate and use those techniques. High risk students need better problem-solving methods, and they must learn as quickly as possible to use them.

6. *Detention.* My mother once told me never to send my kids to bed if they were bad because they would learn that bed is a punishment. What do students learn about school when we tell them that if they are bad, they have to be in school even

longer? Detention is used like prison. Students "serve time." For the high risk child, detention reinforces the idea that the entire school is like prison. Just serving time in school will not help these students. High risk students have already been given hundreds of hours of detention with little or no improvement.

7. *Writing.* Writing essays, paragraphs, or 500 sentences is a commonly used punishment that is exceptionally offensive to someone who loves writing. The effect is that students learn to hate writing. Writing is a wonderful skill and an excellent adventure. It should never be relegated to the status of punishment.

Students at risk typically do not love writing and think of it as a chore. Using writing as a punishment will ruin the chances of their future writing teachers to ever motivate them. If they do like to write, this punishment will destroy the motivation for one of the few activities at which the student might be successful. Either way, writing for punishment is out. Writing for pleasure is in.

The above punishments, like all punishments, fail to have long-lasting effects on behavior. They teach students only not to get caught. Think of the last time you were the recipient of a speeding ticket. After you pulled away from the policeman, did you say to yourself, "I will never speed again," or did you say, "I will never get caught speeding again"? If you are like most drivers, you slowed down for two hours, and after that, you watched for the police.

A "For Better Or Worse" cartoon shows two boys talking. One has been caught swearing and lost television for two weeks. He asks his friend what he is supposed to learn from this. His friend says, "To swear out of earshot."

Punishments fail in the long term for a variety of reasons. One of the most important is that punishments do not elicit a feeling of commitment from students, and without commitment, change in long-term behavior is not possible. Also, punishments anger the recipients and treat them as if they are stupid. For students at risk, these are the exact messages that must be avoided.

THE PRINCIPLE OF ESCALATION

In discipline situations, escalation means that the stakes increase as each side digs in and tries to win. However, when escalation occurs in a school setting, there are no winners. Once escalation begins, all possible rational discussion is over, and the ensuing battle is more like a runaway train than an attempted resolution to a discipline problem.

The best way to avoid escalation is to choose consequences that do not anger, humiliate, embarrass, or demean the student. This is especially true of high risk students. Because they have nothing to lose by continuing the battle, the teacher has almost no leverage in getting them to back down. It does not help to lower their grade or send them home or give them a detention; they have already had those things and are immune to their sting.

If the student should back down and give in to the teacher, then the situation is even worse. Now the student is hurt and blames the teacher. The student will fight the teacher in either outright aggressive or passive aggressive ways. Neither can win.

Power struggles between students and teachers are fruitless, dangerous, unprofessional, and demeaning. They occur when emotions are high. The following steps can defuse a power struggle:

1. *Power struggles get worse if escalated.* When the issue is dignity vs. dignity, it is impossible for either side to back

down. As each side tries to win, they dig in deeper and fight harder, use more weapons, and escalate the struggle.

2. *Neither the student nor the teacher will win.* As the stakes get higher, it becomes more and more impossible for either party to feel like a winner, regardless of how the original issue turns out. The game no longer includes the original issue. It is now based on dignity.

3. *Use active listening.* Teachers using active listening neither agree nor disagree with the student. They acknowledge a student's remarks by paraphrasing them without judging them.

4. *Agree to speak with the student later.* Usually when both parties are angry, it is very difficult to reach any sort of resolution. After trying active listening, set up a time to speak with the student later.

5. *Keep all communication as private as possible.* The presence of other students increases the need of both the teacher and student to win the power struggle. It works to both the teacher's and student's advantage to keep the communication as private as possible and for the teacher not to embarrass the student in front of his peers. Embarrassment will make it harder for the student to resolve things later.

6. *If a student refuses to accept a consequence, use the "insubordination rule."* The insubordination rule should be part of your social contract. It is a bottom line rule that states, "If a student does not accept any consequence, then he is not allowed into the class until he has accepted it." Alternative places for the student are time out, in-school suspension, and out-of-school suspension. Your principal must agree to support this rule, and most do.

Remember that power struggles are emotional battles of will. If your goal is to have the student ready to learn when the struggle is over, you must provide an "out." The student lacks the skill to stop fighting; it requires the professional skill of the teacher to stop. By not fighting with a student, the teacher is a great role model.

---

1. Hembree, Diana, "The Tragic Side of Classroom Punishment," *Hippocrates* (March/April 1989):116.

2. 1986 study by U.S. Department of Education.

Eight

Discipline Methods Need Effective Consequences

Discipline methods work best when they have the following characteristics:

1. *Consequences are clear and specific.* Students must have an idea of what will happen if they break rules. General, vague, or hidden consequences do not help the child learn cause and effect.

2. *Consequences have a range of non-progressive, non-sequenced alternatives.* Both a single consequence for a specific violation and a series of sequenced consequences (for example, first offense is a warning, second offense is a detention, third offense is an in-school suspension) deny the teacher or administrator the ability to match the consequence with the student and the situation. All plans for discipline that remove the judgment of the teacher or administrator are doomed to failure and should be avoided. This is especially true when dealing with the high risk student.

Pre-sequenced programs treat every student the same, just as they treat every teacher the same. These programs are designed to be teacher-proof, meaning "even a teacher can do it," in the same way that fool-proof means, "even a fool can do it." The sequence is based on a single criteria for which consequence is implemented in a discipline situation—the number of times the rule has been violated. It is a one-size-fits-all approach. The hidden reason for pre-sequenced consequences is to protect the system, not help the students.

It is better to choose consequences which will work. Not all consequences work with all children in all situations. With the student at risk, choosing the next consequence in the series will fail just as it always has, and the main messages to the student are: "You are not important here, I can't control you, and no matter how angry you make me feel, I am hopeless in dealing with you. You don't matter."

The case of Charles Rothenberg helps illustrate this point. Rothenberg committed one of the most heinous of all crimes. He poured gasoline all over his young son, David, and lit him on fire. David lived, but is scarred both physically and emotionally. Rothenberg served six years in prison before being paroled the first time. His parole was revoked after a relatively minor offense, but in 1991, he was paroled again. After Rothenberg's first parole, David Kirp wrote the following essay in the *San Francisco Examiner*:

> *Such determinate sentencing rules were inserted into California law in the late 1970s, ironically, in order to prevent liberal judges from setting too short sentences. Politics aside, there are often good reasons to limit the discretion of parole boards and judges: it's a way to protect unpopu-*

> *lar minorities, a way to make sure the legal sys-*
> *tem doesn't become an official lynch mob.*
>
> *Rothenberg's sentence reminds us that rules*
> *aren't always the right answer either. In hard*
> *cases we need to have people making decisions,*
> *not formulas.[1]*

Teachers and administrators must make decisions, not match formulas. Formulas are brainless and have no place in education. Formulas treat children equally, but there are situations where equal treatment is unfair and fair treatment is unequal.

When parents come to school and question why their child was treated differently from other children, explain to them why, by using the following monologue as a guide.

"Thank you for coming in, Mr. and Mrs. Blake. I am glad you are here to talk about your daughter. It is true that I have treated your daughter differently. That is because your daughter is different. She is very special to me. Very unique. My goal is to teach her how to behave responsibly, and I will do anything to help her learn. However, if you think that my method is not appropriate in this case, I will be glad to listen to any suggestions you have. After all, you know your child better than I do. However, there is one thing I will not do. Please do not ask me to treat your child just like everybody else. Your child deserves a lot better than that."

3. *Consequences are related to the rule and are natural or logical.* Rudolf Driekurs[2] did the pioneering work in natural and logical consequences. When consequences are related to the rule violation, the rule violator sees a direct connection between what he does and what happens to him after he does it. Natural consequences teach students responsible ways of behaving. They are especially effective with high risk students

because they diminish the battle between student and teacher, and because they allow the student to see the effects of his behavior.

4. *Consequences protect and maintain the dignity of the student.* The importance of dignity has been discussed previously in this chapter. There is no reason to use any consequence that is humiliating and dehumanizing.

Effective consequences can be natural or logical (related to the rule in a direct manner), conventional (already exist, but are modified for specific situations), generic (apply to all rules), or instructional (designed to teach students how to follow rules).

Following are some examples of each type of effective consequence.

Natural or logical consequences. A middle school shop teacher invented Siberia to solve the problem of students leaving the shop a mess. She borrowed a trunk from the theater department and labeled it "Siberia." When children left their tools around the shop after class, she locked them into Siberia until Friday. To ensure that students could still do their work when their tools were in Siberia, she rented tools to those who were missing theirs. Price of rental: Ten minutes of cleanup after school for each class period of tool rental.

This worked fine and removed the daily cleanup battle between her and her students. But she was still cleaning up, by picking up the tools and depositing them into Siberia. So she had not solved the problem of "those who make the mess clean the mess." Two "Siberian huskies" were elected to monitor cleanup. They patrolled the classroom and made sure all tools were put away. If tools were left out, the huskies put them in Siberia. Everyone wanted to be a husky, so the teacher had to ensure that everyone had a turn before anyone could serve twice.

This magnificent consequence worked beautifully in middle school. I do not think it would have worked in the high school. Every natural consequence must grow out of the specific situation.

Conventional consequences. Common conventional consequences are time out, removal, and suspension. Time out is a technique that has been used successfully for many years by teachers of all grade levels. However, it can be modified to be even more effective by altering the directions related to time served. The goal is to increase the commitment on the part of the student to return to class and be ready to work.

By giving students a set time to remain in time out—for example, five minutes—a golden opportunity is lost to teach students one aspect of behaving responsibly. After the five minutes, they may or may not be ready to return to the classroom. An alternative method is to tell the child: "You have chosen time out. You may return to the class whenever you are ready to learn." If his behavior improves, you have achieved your goal even if the student only serves one minute of time out. If the child elects to stay in time out for an excessive length of time, it is still preferable to having him return before he is ready.

Should the child return before he is ready and continue to misbehave, simply tell him: "It appears you are still not ready. Please return to time out and come back to the classroom activities when you are ready." It helps, at this point, to make a physical connection, such as a gentle touch on the shoulder or a handshake.

Removal from the classroom or suspension is a severe form of time out. It is rare that sending a child to the principal's or vice principal's office for a lecture or intervention will help improve the child's behavior. However, removal from the classroom until the child is ready to learn is often very effective. This technique works especially well when the child and the teacher are both angry and need time apart from each other to cool down. Schools in Essex Junction, Vermont, use both a safe room and a PACS (planning and changing for success) room as alternative forms of in-school suspension. The safe room is for high school students and is staffed by a teacher and an instructional assistant. In the safe room, students can get help with class work or deal with an immediate problem. Students are referred to the PACS room when they are extremely disruptive. In the PACS room, they receive help in developing plans for solving the problem that got them removed from class.

The problem in many schools is often where to send the child. The most logical place to send them is the in-school suspension room if there is one. If not, you can form a partnership with three or four other teachers in your school who will take your students when they need a place to go, in exchange for you taking theirs under similar circumstances. I have seen this technique work with remarkably good results in elementary, middle, and high schools of every type. Without the primary teacher and fellow students to impress or show off for, the students who are removed typically sit in the back of the room quietly until they can return to their classrooms.

This works best when students are not embarrassed or humiliated by where they are sent. Never tell a student: "Since you are acting like a first-grader, you will be a first-grader for the remainder of the day. Report to the first grade at once." Humiliation and ridicule always make the situation worse. Eventually the students will pay you back for hurting their feelings, and there will be an escalation of the battle.

For too many children, out-of-school suspensions mean viewing television and eating junk food at home. Too few parents are at home to supervise their children when they are sent home from school. In-school suspension is a better choice because the children are supervised and do not get a vacation for violating the rules.

Once children are asked to leave the classroom, they need a ticket of admission to return. The ticket is a plan, either oral or in writing, of how they will be ready to begin learning (or behaving) when they get back. The goal is for the students to make some form of commitment to improve their behavior upon returning to the classroom.

Generic Consequences. Four common consequences that can be used for all rules are reminders, warnings, choosing, and planning. There are times with many students when a minor consequence is appropriate and a simple reminder is enough to stop misbehavior. Warnings are firm reminders.

Choosing is a technique that encourages some commitment and internal locus of control. Offer students a choice between three or four alternatives (plans) to solve their behavior problems, and hold them accountable for whichever one they select.

Planning is the most effective consequence that can be used for all rule violations. When students plan their own solutions, there is a high degree of commitment and internal locus of control. It provides the students with a sense of dignity and a feeling of competence. The message to students is that they are capable of behaving differently and that the teacher has faith in them.

Student plans should include the specific steps for changing their behavior; goals alone will not work. Plans should be written, signed, and dated. It often takes three or four attempts for planning to work because students are not used to solving their own problems. I recommend staying with this technique for up to two weeks before giving up on it.

Instructional Consequences. Children often can say exactly what they should do but still not do it. If the reason is that they do not know how, then the solution is to teach them how and to have them practice the new behavior. Musicians and athletes spend hours practicing behavioral skills because simply knowing what to do is not enough. Many children have no experience with certain behaviors, and practice or rehearsing helps a lot.

Whatever type of consequence is used, it must be used well for it to succeed. Following are some suggestions for using consequences in the most effective way possible.

1. Always implement a consequence.

2. Select the most appropriate consequence from your pre-established list.

3. State the rule and consequence to the student. You do not need to say more.

4. Use proximity. Be as physically close to the student as is appropriate.

5. Make direct eye contact. (Watch for cultural exceptions.)

6. Be private. Use a soft, calm voice. Only the student(s) involved should hear.

7. Do not embarrass the student.

8. Be firm, clear, and committed. Strength comes from a commitment that you are doing the right thing, not from the use of force.

9. Be flexible about consequences. Your goal is for the student to improve his/her behavior, not for the student to experience a specific consequence.

10. Do not think in terms of winning and losing. You and your students are both on the same team.

11. Control anger. It is okay to show your students that you are human by expressing genuine anger, but a chronically angry teacher is not effective.

12. Do not accept excuses.

13. Sometimes it is best to let the student choose the consequence.

14. Avoid traps; diffuse power struggles.

15. Avoid behaviors that mark you as a victim. Excessively wimpy or aggressive behavior tells students you are out of control.

16. Alter conditions to reach your goals. Change discipline and classroom structures to help support students to act responsibly.

17. Take a professional stance. Do not interpret student behavior personally.

18. Communication is better than force.

In their book, *Reclaiming Youth At Risk: Our Hope for the Future*, Brendtro, Brokenleg and Van Bockern explain the danger of using negative theories to explain behavior.

> *Novice youth workers often make the mistake of believing the behavior of a difficult youth is directed at them personally. As they learn to see the behavior as a reflection of the youth's personal needs or distress, they are able to disengage from a knee-jerk response of negativism.[3]*

They explain further that when professionals use demeaning or blaming labels, the resulting actions are to avoid/neglect or punish/coerce. However, professionals can use esteeming labels that nurture and empower, or empathizing labels which lead to befriending or encouraging.[4] What a professional does when a child breaks rules depends as much, if not more, on the way that behavior is labeled, as it does upon the behavior itself.

Alex Molnar and Barbara Lindquist use a similar approach to the Discipline with Dignity paradoxical method. They advocate such skills as reframing a problem, looking for positive motivations, and seeing positive functions of problem behavior.[5] An example of reframing is a child who refuses to help around the classroom. A teacher might say, "Ingrid, I appreciate your unselfishness in allowing other students more opportunities to be helpful. That's generous of you because there aren't that many opportunities for everyone." Or when a child does not do his homework, "Thanks, Alphonse. You have given me the opportunity to spend more time giving other students feedback on their papers. That's a generous thing to do."

Molnar and Linquist are very clear that statements like these are not sarcasm, but an honest alternative point of view that the teacher believes. Their research and experience indicate a high degree of success with very difficult youth when using methods like reframing.

The goals are to keep the student close to learning, to keep communication open, and to let the student know that, no matter what he does, even using the big "F" word, there is no sudden death. Hope is not lost. This goal gives me the strength to say something like, "I'm glad you trust me enough to show me your most angry and hateful feelings and to know that no matter how much I dislike it, I will still be there when you need me. That takes a great deal of trust and courage. I appreciate that. It also means that you don't understand or don't care how those words can hurt me. When things cool down, I want to talk to you about this so it won't happen again."

"Behaving paradoxically" in the classroom was developed from Victor Frankl's work in Logotherapy.[6] Frankl found that some people resist changing even when they want to change. He discovered that many people can be helped by having someone strongly suggest that the person continue to behave exactly as he or she has been behaving, and even to exaggerate their maladaptive behavior. This is called "siding with a person's resistance."

1. It can be used with any misbehavior except those that are physically harmful, violations of the law, or destructive of property. You cannot tell a student to hit someone at least once each day.

2. Behaving paradoxically is not to be done with sarcasm. A sarcastic tone will only serve to continue the battle.

3. The other students might wonder why someone is receiving preferential treatment. You can answer by saying, "I don't discuss other students. If you have a concern that you are receiving the wrong amount of (work), then we should discuss it soon." Most students know there has been an ongoing problem with the difficult student and are satisfied to see the tensions relax.

4. Behaving paradoxically is an extreme approach, to be used when nothing else seems to work.

In the classroom, the paradoxical principle can be used as follows:

1. Identify the student for paradoxical. It is probably best to work with only one student at a time. We suggest reserv-

ing paradoxical for those students for whom nothing else has been effective. The problem behavior cannot be abusive, destructive, or harmful to others.

2. Get permission from principal and parent(s) before using paradoxical. An explanation is necessary of why you are using paradoxical, how it will work, and what their role will be.

3. Plan how you will use paradoxical with the child. Set up a simple record-keeping procedure that records the child's responses over time.

4. Remember the principle, "If you take something away, give something back." Plan to find ways of allowing expression of whatever feelings emerge as a result of paradoxical.

   Example: If you stop a child from dumping wastebaskets, he may go on to throwing erasers if you do nothing to deal with his anger about school. Find ways to make school a more positive place to be.

5. Tell the student to continue doing exactly what you had previously been trying to stop.

   Examples:

   a) Your assignment is to not do your homework.

   b) You will have no work to do in this class.

   c) I want you to forget your supplies every day from now on.

   d) I see you want to talk. Let's all listen until you are finished.

   e) From now on, I want you to do your homework for other classes in this class.

6. Notice students' successes. If the student tries what you have told him, commend him for following directions and doing what he was told. If the student defies you, and completes his assignment (for example), then reward him for doing his work. If this sounds paradoxical, that is the point.

7. Be prepared to tell the student why you have given a new message. Example: "I want you to talk out of turn because you do it so well."

8. Do not deliver the message sarcastically, insincerely, or in a challenging manner. If you use paradoxical, then be genuine in the way you speak to your target student.

9. Be prepared to use this method for at least a month, and possibly even longer. Even if the situation stays the same, your life will be easier and so will the student's, because your previous daily struggle will be gone.

---

1. *The San Francisco Examiner,* May 1989.

2. Driekurs, R., *Children: The Challenge* (New York: Hawthorn Books, 1964).

3. Brendtro, Larry, Brokenleg, Martin, and Van Bockern, Steve, *Reclaiming Youth At Risk: Our Hope for the Future* (Bloomington, IN: National Educational Service, 1990) p. 15.

4. Ibid. p. 16-17.

5. Molnar, Alex, and Linquist, Barbara, *Changing Problem Behavior in Schools* (San Francisco: Jossey-Bass, 1990).

6. Frankl, Victor, *Man's Search For Meaning: An Introduction to Logotherapy* (New York: Pocket Books, 1963).

Nine

Altruism

To be of use in this world is the only way to be happy.

— Hans Christian Andersen

W E SPEND SO MUCH TIME TRYING TO HELP high risk students that they subtly receive the message that they must be inferior because they are so needy. One reason that many high risk students are resistant to efforts to help them is that they are rejecting the notion that they are helpless and, therefore, incompetent.

For students with poor academic achievement, the typical classroom is a breeding ground for feelings of incompetence and uselessness. In the last fifteen years, educators have become increasingly aware of the relationship between self-esteem and students' academic performance and social behavior. There are very few educators who have not had some training on the topic of self-esteem. Courses and instructional units have been developed commercially and by school-based task forces to improve the self-esteem of students. It often seems that these programs work best with the students who already have a posi-tive attitude about themselves and are least effective with those students who see themselves the most negatively. The problem is that even sound worksheets and activities simply cannot significantly influence children who continually receive negative messages about themselves. Children are acutely aware of where they stand in the school community and of how they are truly perceived by teachers and other students.

The best way to counter feelings of incompetence and uselessness is to provide opportunities on a regular basis for students to become competent in meeting goals and to become useful. Students need to believe that they matter. Providing opportunities for students to help others meets this need. There are many opportunities in the school for students to be helpful, and more can be created. Schools can go a long way toward changing students' cynical attitudes by systematically developing both formal and informal programs to give students a chance to help others.

Helping others provides an authentic, tangible, direct experience of usefulness. Gratification is immediate. Even if the result of the action is unknown or less than expected, the student knows that he made an effort to care. Helping evokes feelings of connectedness, power, and self-worth.

Because giving and caring are positive values for most people, students who help are viewed as worthwhile and positive by teachers and other students. Even the most cynical, alienated students feel good when others think positively about them.

My son, David, taught me this lesson a few years ago. I was asked to help a group of teachers work through a serious school problem. One of the key teachers called an hour before the meeting and said she couldn't attend because the baby sitter for her four-year-old son cancelled. David saved the day by volunteering to accompany me and to take care of the child at the school site. When we arrived, the child was whining, cranky, and wouldn't leave his mother's side. A number of teachers took turns trying to distract him by making things with the Legos his mother had brought from home.

David intuitively sat beside the boy and asked what the Legos were. David knew what Legos were—he has had enough of them in his life to build a replica of the Golden Gate Bridge. The child said, "You build things with them." David asked if he would show him how to build something. For the duration of the meeting, the child taught David how to make things with Legos.

Why was the child resistant to learning about Legos, but eager to teach about them? Because, as a teacher, he was useful, competent, important, and in control. The same phenomenon applies to high risk children in school. Helping provides the opportunity to be top dog for a change. It is an extremely powerful tool in the overall context of reaching the unreachable child.

HELPING VERSUS POSITIVE REINFORCEMENT

Realistically, providing opportunities for students to help will not miraculously transform them into model citizens who excel academically. But it *will* influence their attitudes about themselves and about their role in school.

For example, Al Mendler, my colleague, works a couple of times a month in a secured home for juvenile delinquents, teenagers convicted of criminal acts. He describes how difficult it is to reach many of the hard cases, especially those who came from the streets of New York City. One of the most successful strategies he uses involves the concept of helping. He brings in professional clowns who teach the residents how to dress and act like clowns. The clowns-in-training then dress in costumes and makeup and perform for hospitalized children.

The patients love the clowns. They appreciate them and laugh with them. The students feel needed and appreciated. There have been no incidents of inappropriate behavior by the clowns when out of the home. Mendler reports that their behavior improves for significant lengths of time and that it is much easier to discuss their problems with them.

Another example involves Bill, a sixth-grade student in a rural community, who fought frequently, was surly, and did little work. The best way to describe his home life was toxic: alcoholic mother, father in jail, few friends. He already had started drinking heavily in times of stress.

The principal, school counselor, and teachers decided to help Bill feel useful by giving him a major helping responsibility. The school had a first-grader who was confined to a wheelchair, and Bill was assigned the task of helping the first-grader on and off the bus every day. Bill was also assigned to be the first-grader's protector. The only stipulation was that if Bill had a fight, he could not help the first-grader for the remainder of the week.

Bill took his assignment very seriously and watched over the younger child like a mother hawk over her chicks. The children became friends, and one day when the younger student was ill, a teacher saw a tear coming out of Bill's previously hardened eyes. Bill did not become a model student. He still fought on occasion, and he struggled academically. But his attitude changed significantly. Someone was depending on him, and he felt needed, important, and loved. This experiment opened a new door for Bill, one he desperately needed.

Vicki Hartzig is a first-grade teacher in Michigan. After attending a Discipline with Dignity workshop, she thought of how helping might benefit a rowdy fourth-grade student in her school. He was typically slovenly dressed, swore voraciously, and refused to try even the simplest assignment. When his teacher gave him a class assignment, he typically gave it back and said he wouldn't do it, no matter what.

After careful negotiations with the boy's teacher and the principal, who were reluctant, at first, to reward negative behavior with a "positive" opportunity, Vicki invited the boy into her first-grade class to tutor any students who needed help, once every day. She told him he could come as long as he was relatively neat, did not swear, and caused no problems with her students. If none of her students needed help, he could sit quietly and do his schoolwork until he was needed.

Within a week, the first-graders cheered when he entered the room. They fought over who he would help first. He began combing his hair and tucking in his shirt before entering the room. He was always polite and friendly. One day, after struggling to teach a concept to a first-grader, he told Mrs. Hartzig, "Boy, being a teacher is harder than I thought." His regular teacher noticed a distinct change in his attitude. At first, he still did little work, but was not rude or mean. Later, he began trying his assignments. He even asked for help when he didn't understand how to do something.

An experiment that has been tried in California, and is now spreading to other areas of the country, uses the principle of helping with tough adolescents in alternative schools and homes. Many of these adolescents have been involved with gangs. On a regular basis, these youths are brought to geriatric nursing homes and homes for physically disabled youngsters to read stories, to help with exercise, in some cases to feed, and in general, to just do what they can to be helpful.

The results have been dramatic. Significant changes in attitudes and behaviors have occurred for a majority of the youths in the program. They have formed close attachments with the people they help and are very protective of them. They go out of their way to be supportive and encouraging. They listen to problems and offer advice or suggestions. They enthusiastically report for duty on their assigned days and have been reliable. Not only have their attitudes about their roles in the nursing homes and hospitals changed, but their future hopes and plans have also been influenced. Many now say they want to go into a "helping" profession when they grow up.

These examples clearly demonstrate the power of helping. When students are given the responsibility to be caretakers, tutors, and helpers of people in need, they respond responsibly. They begin to feel useful and important. They find that others depend on them, and they flourish in it.

No longer do the labels, "useless," "incompetent," or "high risk," apply. The change comes not from discussions or activities about self-concept, but from real life. Those who are helped do not see the students as failures, and the labels become inappropriate. Teachers use the labels less, and the attitudes of all concerned are forced to adjust. Change of attitude leads to hope.

CREATING HELPING OPPORTUNITIES

There are a wide variety of helping opportunities that exist naturally in schools. Others can be created with a little careful planning. Students can tutor other students or become hall, bathroom, or playground monitors. They can also perform for the other students.

The clowns-in-training program referred to above is an example. Students can read or act to lower grade students as well as to their peers. Performing might also include creating school or classroom-related artwork, such as posters, signs or decorations.

They can help both teachers and administrators by performing many administrative or secretarial tasks, such as taking attendance, collecting papers, making phone calls in the office, running duplicating machines, delivering written messages, collating, or answering phones. High risk students can be given leadership positions on student task forces that suggest solutions for school or classroom problems. They can help raise money for school programs or charity. They can assist disabled students or become big brothers/sisters to younger students.

The big brother/sister program can be modeled in a school. Some target students might have had the advantage of big brothers or sisters themselves and have a good understanding of how to behave in this role. Bring in community service experts who work in the big brother/sister program to help you set up the program for your school and to teach big brother/sister skills to the target students.

There are also opportunities for students to help outside of the school. Time can be found before school and during free time in the school day. Some possible sources for these opportunities are nursing homes, homes for disabled youngers, recreational parks or arenas, shut-ins, elderly people who need help shopping, and day-care centers.

The characteristics of opportunities that are the most helpful are:

1. *The opportunity is genuine.* Artificial situations will be perceived as phony and will not encourage students to become involved. It is hard to disguise an artificial situation to look genuine. Students quickly see through the rhetoric and respond cynically. Make sure that the opportunity is real.

2. *The opportunity involves tasks that match the ability of the student.* Not all students have the ability to be helpful in

the same way, so do not ask students to do a task that will most likely lead to failure. On the other hand, be careful not to pick demeaning chores that are far beneath the student's ability. If a child has a specific skill or ability, try to use it in a helping task. Sometimes students can resolve their own problems by helping others with the same problem. If the student has a problem in a particular area, that can be the basis for a successful helping experience with lower-level students. For example, if a student has trouble reading, he or she might benefit by tutoring younger students in that subject. Students who are loud in the hall often make good hall monitors. Students who fight on the playground can often stop others from fighting. Because they understand the problem from a different perspective, sometimes they can be more effective than teachers. In the process, they learn to see their own behavior from a different perspective.

3. *The opportunity is optional.* Do not force a student to help. Not only will this increase resistance, but it will minimize the healing effect. The student will have trouble taking credit for what he does if he was required to do it.

4. *The opportunity is not broadcast to others.* Keep the activity low-key, especially at first. Be appreciative without praising. Do not publicly announce what is going on. The goal of helping is to give the student an internal feeling of worth; public praise or acknowledgement may sound helpful, but it will shift the feeling of worth to an external reward. This will cheapen the experience, and the opportunity may backfire. If you want to acknowledge your appreciation to the student, do it privately and as simply as possible.

Eventually, if the student is clearly feeling competent and useful, it might be possible to publicly honor him or her for what he or she has done. This is best done in a social context where many students are honored. It is important to keep the pressure off a student in the formative stages of helping. The student still doubts whether or not he can succeed, and undue public praise will only make the "inevitable" fall that much more crushing.

5. *The opportunity does not work if it rewards negative behavior.* One of the major objections to providing these opportunities is that educators fear they reward negative behavior. "Why let the kids who break the rules and who are always in trouble get to do something rewarding and fun?" they ask.

It is more important to worry about what can be done to prevent future misbehavior and to turn around the attitudes of the high risk students than it is to worry about whether or not they may enjoy school too much. Rewarding negative behavior is unimportant and trivial compared to the good these opportunities can do. Giving high risk students the opportunity to be helpful will not induce the "good kids" to behave badly because they want to be treated the same way. In fact, all students should be given the opportunity to be helpful.

6. *The opportunity is one of a variety of possibilities.* Develop a number of different kinds of helpful activities to meet a variety of needs. Some can occur once a week, others every day. Some can occur on the school site; others can involve the entire community. Some can earn academic credit; others can be very informal.

7. *The opportunity provides enough time for positive results to occur.* Do not expect instant results. Give the healing effect of helping a reasonable period of time to occur, at least a month or two. As long as things are not getting worse, stay with the process, even though it might appear that it is not making a difference.

8. *The opportunity ensures that those being helped want to be helped.* If the intended recipients do not wish to be helped or are resistant to being helped by the student selected, it is better to abort the attempt than it is to force the situation. A resistant recipient will most likely communicate to the helper that he is not welcome. That is precisely the feeling this technique is designed to reduce.

There is nothing wrong with requiring students to earn the privilege of helping by meeting reasonable standards of behavior. Students can be expected to temporarily lose the privilege of helping if they fight or behave in other unacceptable ways.

When setting up expectations, make sure that they are tailored to the individual student. Do not require a student to do something that is beyond his ability nor require a student to do something he has never done before. Be flexible about expectations. Alter them upward or downward to respond to results. The goal is to use the helping opportunity as motivation to alter behavior, not to screen out potential helpers. For the same reason, make sure that other administrators or teachers do not screen out students for the wrong reasons. Get as many students as possible into helping situations.

Begin with expectations that are light, and gradually increase them if the student shows progress. When a student fails to meet the expectations, keep the time he is removed from the helping situation short. A period of a day or two should deliver the message. Get the students back as quickly as possible. Take care not to reinforce negative labeling when disciplining the student. The message of the reprimand should focus on the student's mistake and not on whether the student is worthy of being a helper.

Ten

Competition and Students at Risk

The only competition worthy of a wise man is with himself.

— Washington Allston

COMPETITION IS AN INTEGRAL PART of school life. Students compete not only in athletics but also for grades, the honor roll, and the teacher's attention. There is social competition: gaining entry to cliques and gangs, collecting friends, being the best dressed, or being the most "cool." For those who do not win at games condoned by the school, there are other contests: who can get his name on the board the most times, who can get thrown out of the class the most often, who can collect the most detentions, and who can fail the most tests. Sometimes the competition is between the teacher and student, fighting for power and control.

Children are not strangers to competition when they first come to school. They have had many experiences at home in both formal and informal games. However, school is the first place where they encounter competition with relative strangers, and where they must play the games for stakes that powerful adults consider important. Their successes and failures are recorded and sent home. If they are winners, they are rewarded. If they fail, they are losers.

Some losers find ways to protect themselves. They disregard the value of the games. They disrupt the games so others have difficulty playing. They find other games to play in which they can win. They fail on purpose to soften the blow. Some losers are not that good at protection. They accept themselves as failures. Because they are unsuccessful in the social arena, they seek out others like themselves for friends, and reinforce in each other in various protection strategies.

The competitive nature of school produces winners and losers. Because there is such a diverse number and many kinds of competitive outlets, there can be many winners. But there are some who rarely win. The students we label at risk are losers in one or more major competitive situations that are valued highly by the school. They are failures in the game of academics.

There are two strongly held and contradictory views about the nature of competition and its role in education. The first is that competition begins early and lasts a lifetime. Babies compete with their siblings for parental attention, toys, and control of the household. The elderly find competition a healthy and fun way to recreate; they play cards, backgammon, mah-jongg, and bingo. Companies compete with each other for customers, and employees within companies compete with each other for top positions. High school, college, and professional sports have elevated competition to an expensive high art that provides entertainment for millions. When non-competitive games are invented, like throwing a frisbee, players find a way to turn them into competitive battles. Competition is intrinsic to the American way of life.

Competition provides challenge, which elevates performance. It provides team spirit and the ability to work with others to achieve common goals. It rewards sustained effort and teaches the value of working hard to achieve both short- and long-term objectives. It teaches the value of practice and of paying attention to details. Competition is a proving ground for developing leadership and learning how to follow directions. Competition is naturally motivating, stimulating, and fun.

The second view, also held by many educators, is that competition can be harmful. They point out that competition does not always teach teamwork, but sometimes generates jealousy, anger, blaming, and power struggles for leadership. Competition can lead to cheating. Recent political campaigns have become increasingly dirty and foul. Sports competition often treats players as commodities, to be bought and used. Abuses in college recruiting for big time sports are out of control. The widespread cheating and abuses among NCAA athletic teams have forced college presidents (the Knight Commission) to draft resolutions to limit the power of athletic departments.

When the need to win becomes strong enough, it can cause normally rational people to behave in extremely irrational ways. When fans yell "kill the ump," it is usually a figure of speech. However, Curtis Fair of East St. Louis took it literally when he picked up a bat and went after a teenage umpire of a boys league baseball game, threatening to kill him.[2] And competition destroys the self-concept of the losers. Many educators fear that emphasizing competition as part of the learning process will emphasize all of the dangers and actualize few of the benefits.

The problem with these two views of competition is that both are half right. Competition is a natural part of human nature, but that does not mean that all competitive situations are healthy. Competition can both increase and decrease motivation, productivity, team work, and self-concept. What separates helpful from destructive forms of competition are the goals, the control of participation, and the active support of a hopeful attitude in the participants.

In order to understand competition, we must consider how it relates to the development of positive self-concepts, to learning, and to the student at risk.

There are four major factors which interplay in any competition:

1. Whether participation in the activity is voluntary or required.

2. Whether the emphasis of the competition is on playing or winning.

3. Who controls the structure of the activity and enforces the rules.

4. Whether the activity has the ability to generate a hopeful attitude.

Each of these factors has certain implications for personal development.

Voluntary competition is better than involuntary competition for the student. Each student is usually the best judge of whether to enter a competition. Without coercion to compete, students can choose competitions that do not threaten them, thus protecting their self-concept if they lose.

Examples of voluntary competition in regular classroom situations include cases where students may choose instructional groups on the basis of interest, where the classroom provides a variety of learning activities for student selection, and where no student is ever pressured to participate in a particular classroom activity. Common examples of involuntary competition include cases where all students take the same exam at the same time, where everyone must participate in the same events or activities, and where students are grouped without choice by ability for instructional and prestige purposes.

When it is more important to win a competition than it is to just play, a climate is created that encourages cheating, cutting corners, and general distrust. This creates unhealthy attitudes that actually hinder learning and the personal growth of students.

When it is more important to win, the competition is *ends-centered*. Examples of ends-centered competition include classrooms where report cards are sent home with letter grades; where achievement charts are displayed for spelling, math, and reading; and where praise and criticism are selectively distributed by the teacher.

Ends-centered competition is costly to winners and losers alike. The long-term prognosis for the losers in ends-centered competitions is danger. For those students already at risk, negative self-concepts are reinforced and the alienation and desire to escape escalates.

When students can play the game without the threat of failure, the competiton is *means-centered*. Examples of means-centered competition include classrooms where no external rewards or punishments are granted for academic achievement, where non-comparative feedback is provided for all student work, and where students are allowed to progress at their own rate.

Means-centered competitive activities downplay winning and make playing or participating the central goal. By focusing on the activity rather than the outcome, students can look at the results as feedback for improving performance; and the results of the activity do not label a student's capabilities.

The third factor, control, is not as critical as the first two. If participation is voluntary and the activity is means-centered, competition will most likely be positive when the teacher establishes and enforces the rules. However, there are some potential negative effects on students if the teacher does keep control of the competition. For example, it may promote moral irresponsibility, especially in learning situations. Students learn the attitude, "It's okay to do something wrong as long as I don't get caught." Students gain the chance to develop moral integrity by owning the responsibility for enforcing the rules.

Examples of activities in which the students can develop moral integrity include those in which students share responsibility for evaluating their work, in which each individual is responsible for not cheating, and in which each player is responsible for maintaining the rules in classroom games.

When the teacher maintains control, students miss the opportunity to learn responsibility. One example is when only the teacher's criteria are used in evaluating students' work; (the teacher gives an exam, grades it, and returns it to the student). Other examples include the common situations in which the responsibility for preventing cheating is exclusively the teacher's, and in which the teacher always maintains the rules in classroom games.

Providing activities that generate hopeful attitudes is perhaps the most important factor, yet it is the most elusive to describe. When a competition creates hope, it encourages a student to try harder to achieve. The student believes that with additional effort or with the attainment of additional skills, he can do better. Students are not encouraged to be hopeful when they are continually compared to more successful students or when they have only one chance to succeed or fail. And when students are labeled by the results of the activity, regardless of whether the label is positive or negative, they become cynical.

Both teachers and other students determine the attitudes that are generated during an activity. Thus, it is very important for the teacher to model encouraging, non-labeling behavior and to teach all students to do the same. The teacher must be careful to notice how hard students try, as well as how much they accomplish and how fast they accomplish it. Leadership roles in competitive activities can be shared with all students.

Social competition is another area where an effective teacher can help. Schools have always tried, with little success, to break down social groups, a task that really is beyond any school or teacher. But teachers can create opportunities for children to be in teams with members of different cliques. Whether or not exposure to different students will change attitudes and encourage new friendships, it will at least open the door. The following is an example of how grading fits within these four factors:

CLASSROOM COMPETITION—GRADING

1. Is involuntary

Students have no choice of how, or if, they are to be graded. The school and teacher determine the grading policy for all students, leaving them no alternative but to compete academically.

2. Is ends-centered

By their very nature, grades stress ends rather than means. Grades encourage students to concentrate on rewards (or punishments) rather than on learning.

3. Is system-controlled

The responsibility of enforcing the grading system rests solely on the teacher. The pressure put on students to succeed causes cheating, dropping out (physically as well as intellectually and emotionally), and undue stress for students and teachers alike.

4. Creates hopeless attitudes

Grades categorize and document student achievement, and become predictors for future achievement. Bad grades are recorded lists of failure. Good grades pressure some students to do anything to maintain them. They stigmatize and confine students by labeling them according to ill-defined and subjective criteria which reflect the evaluation skills of the teacher as much as the performance skills of the student. Grades reduce hopeful attitudes by locking in on assessment of the future based on the recorded past.

An example of how the pressure affects even the best students can be found in courses in which pre-med students are vying for top grades. The article "Medicine: Cutthroat Pre-Meds" points to the issue of competition and the quality of doctors which may result from the fierce competition for admission to medical schools. The article contends that "at many universities, pre-med students are engaged in a sort of academic guerrilla war to assure not only higher grades for themselves, but also lower grades for their competing classmates. The result is an unhealthy atmosphere that could have hurt the quality of American Medicine."[3]

Students will "dry-lab" (fake results of) scientific experiments, cheating on examinations is widespread, and students sabotage each other to get good grades, despite harsh penalties for such acts.[4]

Many systems of assessing students' progress are available to the teacher. Those systems of evaluation emphasize more student control in the process, more emphasis on effort than achievement, and more self and peer grading. (See Chapter 11 for more information on grading.)

SELF-CONCEPT

Competition that most likely contributes to the development of positive self-concept includes one or more (preferably more) of the following factors: voluntary participation, means emphasis, internal control, and an orientation to hope. Conditions of participation and emphasis are factors which greatly affect the self-concept.

Deciding to compete means making choices based on a personal assessment of the outcomes. When students see the outcomes as safe, or at least not threatening, to their esteem, the event is attractive. On the other hand, when students are coerced or forced to compete without sufficient knowledge of the consequences, deleterious effects on self-concept are possible. In competition, when means are emphasized, students usually compete with themselves so that the rewards are plentiful and immediate and, therefore, very likely to bolster their self-concept. Together, voluntary participation and an emphasis on means make the strongest combination for building positive self-concepts.

TEACHING STRATEGIES AND COMPETITION

The strategies used by the teacher influence what competitions exist in the classroom. Classroom strategies are counterproductive when they set up competition in which students must participate, the ends are stressed, the teacher is the judge of student progress, and the poorest students have little reason to hope. Some examples are:

The Right Answer. When teachers use a strict, right-answer approach, they require students to compete by having the correct answers to gain the attention of the teacher or peers. Students have no choice but to compete; the right answers are the ultimate ends; and the teacher is the judge.

The Teacher-Centered, Task-Oriented Classroom. In this classroom, students work "independently" to meet teacher-derived goals; each student gains some reward for getting work done. In these classrooms, it is very common to see a chart of various tasks (for example, spelling levels) with each student's name and check marks or stars to mark the child's progress. This is a form of competition in which the teacher determines the tasks (ends), and the teacher judges the student's progress.

The Review. Reviews consist of discussions that require students to repeat what they have learned. Only certain students are involved in the discussions—the ones who did their assignment. Teachers who spend most of their time reviewing are unaware that students who are made to look stupid in front of their classmates have lost in a serious form of public competition: who is the smartest.

Demonstrations. Students usually sit and react to their teachers' demonstrations. When appropriate, certain students are selected to be involved. The most dangerous aspect of demonstrations is that they inadvertently set up a competition between the students and teachers.

Grouping. Students are placed in groups for the purpose of instruction in reading, math, social studies, language arts, and science. Students are forced to compete to be in the best group. Students also compete for their teachers' affection and the other informal perks of being in the best groups. These perks are usually subtle: smiles, arms on shoulders, more tolerance, and other forms of caring; but they are very powerful. Students continually compete to get them, until they realize they have no chance. When all hope is lost, they prefer to be in the lowest group so that there is no pressure.

All classroom activities can be adapted to use positive aspects of competition. Teachers truly can be facilitators rather than controllers. Learning activities are designed around the students' interests and needs. Learning is perceived in terms of growth, the increased ability of students to accept responsibility, to make informed decisions, and to recognize their own individuality and independence in concert with the individuality and independence of others. Understanding what information means and how it is used is more important than simply obtaining a prescribed amount of factual knowledge. Competition exists, but it is positive and growth-producing

Academic Games. Another common classroom strategy, so fraught with competition that it deserves special consideration, is the use of games. Games, like teaching styles, can establish competition that either supports or impedes growth and learning. The problem with academic games is not the competition, which can provide a healthy challenge and increase motivation for most students. Problems occur when all students must participate. That makes the "slower" students look foolish and attacks their dignity. This danger can be avoided by allowing students to choose to play or to do a different activity, alone or in a smaller group, that meets the same objective as the game. If the other students are having fun and the dangers are low, the slower students might decide to join in and take the risk. This is most likely to happen as they increase their skills by doing individual learning games.

The second danger is that winning in these games can get out of control. As long as the pressure to win is controlled—

just enough to encourage trying, but not enough to discourage the losers from wanting to play again—the games can be fun.

Social Games. These games are usually unconscious and involve the class in the most subtle form of competition. They occur when teachers favor certain students or behaviors, and the resulting competition is for the teacher's approval. On the surface, student involvement in these games appears to be voluntary; however, there is a great degree of coercion used to get the students involved.

Behavior Games. Behavior management, contingency contracting, and performance contracting are often used as part of an overall discipline plan. A common procedure involves a token economy; students earn tokens for performing certain approved actions, and these tokens can be cashed in for rewards. Students have no choice but to become involved, the rewards are the ends, and the teacher is the judge of how many rewards there are and who deserves them. Hope is based on how successfully a student gathers the bounty.

While most of the games mentioned above can be altered for positive growth, other kinds of games exist that almost naturally promote positive competition. Appropriately-used simulation games are good examples. Simulation games stress means rather than ends. Winning is not nearly as important as the process of playing and discussing the results. Students can choose to become involved or to be observers. Often, students are involved in establishing and maintaining the rules governing the simulation.

Any competition can be converted to promote meaningful learning and growth. The first step is to identify the different types of competition that exist in an individual classroom. The above list represents possible classroom competitive situations, yet each classroom has its own unique characteristics. Teachers can list the competitions they use and analyze them to see their relative effects. With the help of students, colleagues, or administrators, teachers can revise or design competitions to provide the maximum benefits from each activity.

Notice this example:

Leah is a fifth-grade teacher who used a learning academic quiz game to review social studies facts. Most students loved the activity, and often asked her if they could play. The sessions were lively and fun. However, five of the students were reluctant to participate. The other students moaned when these students were assigned to their team. They tended to give stupid answers, which elicited sarcasm from their teammates. Occasionally, these exchanges escalated into shouting matches. When the teams received grades, these students received low marks for both their contributions to the team effort and for their wrong answers.

Leah, whose intention was to motivate students and make social science fun, had inadvertently created an involuntary activity that focused on ends and diminished hope for the students who were at risk. Once she understood what was truly happening, she changed the game. Her modifications were designed to make the activity voluntary, to focus on means, to let the students control the game, and to increase the hopefulness of all students. She also desired to change the focus of the activity from learning facts to understanding concepts.

In her new game, she set up teams of advisors to solve historical problems. She handed out fact sheets, so no one was required to memorize them. Each team had recorders, chairpersons, advisors, researchers, and enablers. The problems required analysis and higher-level problem solving. "Given the relationship between these countries, and given their resources, what's the best way for them to distribute water, food, and raw materials?"

Students could choose to work in a group, or work alone if they desired. A third choice was to read a book related to the problem and write a report. Students were allowed to suggest alternative projects if they desired, and she would allow them if they were related. One student, who had low verbal skills but high artistic talent, made a wall-size mural depicting the raw materials of each country.

No one complained—everyone won, including Leah. The new game focused on problem solving. It was voluntary, means-centered, run by students, and was hopeful for the entire class. And the students still asked to play just as often.

It is primarily the teacher's responsibility to ensure that competitions are positive experiences for students. By choosing competitive structures that are voluntary, means-centered, internally-controlled, and build hopeful attitudes, the teacher can reap many of the rewards of competition while avoiding most of the harm.

1. *Sports Illustrated*, 27 May 1991, p. 21.

2. *Time*, 20 May 1974, p. 62.

3. Ibid.

4. Ibid.

5. Berne, Eric, *Games People Play* (New York: Grove Press, 1964).

Eleven

How Grading Affects Hope

I don't know why every American can't be above average.

— Dwight David Eisenhower

THE MOST PROMINENT EXAMPLE OF COMPETITION in the classroom is conventional grading. By every factor discussed in the last chapter, conventional grading is destructive. Students have no choice about whether, or how, they will be graded. Grades force students to concentrate on the ends, the grades, rather than on learning. Grading is controlled entirely by the teacher. Conventional grading destroys hope by stigmatizing those who lose. As long as grades maintain their importance, all students will be profoundly affected by them; and those who do poorly will be affected the most. It is sad that most parents and educators place more value on mere grades than on actual learning.

The proponents of traditional grading claim that grades provide a simple system that is clear to everyone. A "B" means "B," and everyone can understand that. Grades provide critical information for making comparisons among students; and they provide a source of control to the school community, maintaining the structure necessary for academic discipline. Grades prepare students for the real world, where they will be judged and "graded" by their employers, friends, and significant others. With the removal of grades, chaos would ensue.

Grades have value only if they are reliable and accurate. One aspect of reliability is whether the same work will receive the same grade no matter who scores the test. However, it has long been known that most tests do not have this kind of reliability. More than 50 years ago, Daniel Starch and Edward Elliot studied the reliability of grading in high school English and math. They gave the same tests to 142 English teachers who taught at the same level. They also gave the same geometry test to 138 geometry teachers to check math. The grades for the English paper ranged from scores of 64 to 98 for the same paper; the math grades varied even more, with scores ranging from 28 to the mid-90s.[1]

Another aspect of reliability is that grades must predict future success. Those students who get good grades should do well in related areas later in life, and those who get poor grades should do poorly later in life. This aspect of reliability is the entire basis for using grades as a screening device. However, there is little evidence that grades have high predictive value. There is more evidence to show that grades do not predict future success very well.

Closely related to reliability is the issue of objectivity. Many educators assume that it is possible for them to grade fairly because they are detached, because they treat all students the same, because they account for individual differences, or because they use a numerical system. Actually, any one system of determining grades is biased because its goals and procedures are based on the perceptions of the teacher using them.

This can be understood more easily by looking at the different criteria teachers use to determine what is worth a good grade. Some teachers give points in essay tests for each correct response covered in the answer; others consider style an important factor; some count spelling and punctuation; and others consider length. In math, there are teachers who give credit only for correct answers; others give credit for the correct process, even if the answer is incorrect; while others give credit only for using the proper format. Neatness is often a factor for some teachers and not for others.

The definition of good work depends on the intent of the evaluator. In most cases, the students who perform the best are those who have successfully deduced the teacher's purposes. Even when the teacher has overtly specified his purposes, performance is evaluated subjectively.

Although many teachers are uncomfortable with grades, most are convinced that they cannot do without them. Grades give teachers power and control over the classroom. Teachers can use grades as a powerful weapon to control both learning and behavior. Students who do not learn what the teacher has decided is worth learning have their actions recorded permanently through grades. Once a student receives a low or failing grade, there is often no way to remove it from the record.

Mistakes are permanent. Permanent records, aided by the use of computers, enable grades to follow students from school to school, to admissions offices and employers, and presumably to the grave. "Here lies Bill McGee. He was only worth a C."

The power of grades is a double-edged sword. As long as a student cares about grades, the teacher can use them to control behavior and influence motivation, at least to some degree. If a student does not care about the grade, then the teacher loses that control and influence. Students without hope already know their grades before they receive their report cards. Because their academic history is low, they cannot be controlled or motivated by grading. So a paradox is created: those students the teacher most wants to motivate and whose behavior is the most difficult to control are least affected by grades. Grades do little to help either high risk students or their teachers.

Students who do poorly in the grading game behave in three basic ways to cope with their failure. One is to drop out. There are staggering statistics that tell us the number of students who physically drop out, but there is no way of knowing how many psychological dropouts there are in every class. Psychological dropouts are students who will not take the risks necessary to learn.

A second way of coping with failure is to accept the low grades as a true measure of their worth. The student in this second category has adopted the self-fulfilling prophecy of failure.

The third common behavior of students who get poor grades is cheating. There is little motivation for the student at risk to cheat; their expectations for academic success are low, and they do not care a great deal about grades. Yet students at risk still cheat. They do so because cheating is fun and stimulating. They can win respect and be noticed by classmates when they get away with cheating, yet the stakes are low; getting caught cannot greatly harm them or discredit them. Finally, cheating is a way to get their teachers off their backs. If they can score reasonably well, they can avoid lectures and scoldings.

Grades can generate enough anxiety to place good academic students at risk. It prevents them from stretching their learning muscles. My friend, Bob, taught math in an upper middle-class suburb, teaching a highly motivated seventh-grade class. The students' parents were already thinking of status colleges, and the pressure on the students to succeed was intense. When Bob took over the classroom, there was a high incidence of cheating, an observation that was readily, almost proudly, verified by the students.

After much frustration because of the cheating, Bob tried an experiment. He told the class that he abhorred cheating, and he could not teach when cheating occurred. He would rather give an A than have anyone cheat. The new rule was that if anyone wanted a good grade so much as to cheat, Bob would give that person an A with no questions asked. However, if a student took a test or handed in a paper, he or she had to do so without cheating. The first paper assigned under this system brought five requests for A's; the next brought three, all from different students. Finally, the third and all subsequent assignments brought no requests for A's. Simultaneously, the evidence of cheating diminished, and the students, apparently quite honestly, confessed that it wasn't worth cheating anymore.

While I do not recommend this method as a universal solution, it is an illustration of how to focus students on learning rather than on achieving good grades.

Susan Wyatt discusses whether grades help or hinder learning as follows:

> *Burke conducted a study with students at the University of Minnesota. His results showed that 7.9% of the students thought grades helped learning, 65.8% thought grades interfered with learning, and 26.3% were undecided. Those who considered grades helpful based their reasons on a need for extrinsic motivation, the lack of*

self-discipline and self-determined goals, and an unwillingness to study "dull" material unless coerced. Essentially, they lacked the internal motivation to learn. Those who claimed that grades interfered with learning provided a wide range of reasons:

1. *The extreme importance attached to "good" grades results in grades, not knowledge or learning, becoming the prime interest of students.*

2. *Grades are not the real value of a course; its real value lies in use and application of what is learned later on in life.*

3. *Emphasis on grades makes students take courses in which they can get good grades instead of courses in which they are interested and would like to take.*

4. *Grades handicap teachers, requiring them to teach things they can measure. Teachers are no longer seen as a "helpers" but as critics.*

5. *Grades create the frustration of receiving bad grades.*

6. *Students learn only what they feel will be on the test and do their best to out-guess the teacher.*

7. *Students are afraid to make mistakes, appear stupid, or displease the instructor.*

8. *Grades drive students to dishonest behavior in school.*

9. *Grades force class attendance and encourage memorizing and cramming for the test followed by eventual forgetting.*

Consequently, many students prefer to separate their academic experience from their actual learning.[2]

TRUST AND GRADING

Grading generally reduces trust in the classroom. Grading is a judgment placed upon the student that inhibits risk-taking and openness. If the stakes are high enough, as they often are in graded systems, the students opt for the safety of prescribed behavior, instead of new, untested behaviors which might prove too risky. Further, because of the high degree of negative competitiveness associated with grades, the students tend not to be open and accepting of each other. Students who cooperate with peers might not do as well as the peers they helped. Students learn to be critically selective of those they trust. The final result is a classroom where students have little trust for each other or for the teacher.

CHANGING YOUR CLASSROOM GRADING SYSTEM

When I was teaching a seminar course in college, I tried to find a way to modify my course evaluation procedure. I gave my students the final examination on the first day of class. It was due on the last day. The exam had fifteen questions related to teaching, each based upon a procedure required of any teacher. Examples included: "What is your grading procedure?" "What is your discipline plan?" "What is your plan for motivating hard-to-reach students?" The students had the option of adding up to three new questions if none of my fifteen were relevant to their particular teaching assignments. They also had the option of creating a different evaluation format if the examination made no sense to them whatsoever (I had to approve any new format in advance). Four questions answered correctly earned a B, six earned an A. The students could submit any answer to me at any time during the semester for review and feedback. The students felt that the test took their needs as learners into account, and I believe that it met my needs as a teacher who wanted my students prepared to teach.

Changing the grading system will help all students. It will help restore hope for those students who have lost it, and it will help increase their willingness to risk more of themselves in the learning process. Changing the grading system will also help prevent other students from reducing the amount of risk they are willing to take as learners; and keep them from becoming hidden high risk students, those who get good grades but do not learn.

Following are some of the alternatives to the conventional grading system.

Alternative One: Self-Grading

This first alternative simply allows the students to determine their own grades. The teacher can supply the criteria and data for the student to use in deciding the grade; or the student can determine criteria, within guidelines, for a given course of study. How much student input is desired depends on the ability of students to comprehend this task. Young children, when given guidelines and examples, are more adept at this process than most teachers assume. Older students need to overcome the desire either to beat the system with inflated grades or to downgrade themselves with unrealistically low grades. In fact, studies indicate that students tend to give themselves lower, rather than higher, grades when allowed to grade themselves. The benefit of this alternative is that students are encouraged to evaluate their own work; and although translating their work into a grade is still not ideal, at least the student is involved in the process.

One pitfall of this system is that students without experience in self-evaluation have adjustment problems. These can be minimized by gradually introducing self-grading, but for some students, the adjustment still will be difficult. Another pitfall is that your students might all choose A's. If you record them, your administration might not be too pleased; and if you refuse to give the high grades chosen by the students, they might lose their trust in you. Either way, the system falls apart.

Furthermore, I personally have experienced discomfort in self-grading when a student selects a grade either too high or too low in my estimation. If you are constantly feeling this frustration, self-grading might not be an answer for you. I have gotten over my feelings by reminding myself that as long as grades exist, any system we use is disconcerting. But the negative feelings in self-grading are minimal, especially in light of the benefits.

Robert Leeper says of his experiences with self-grading:

> *For me, the most exciting experiences I have had with students took place in classes where grades were dispensed with by making it clear at the first meeting that the students could grade themselves, where there were no fixed requirements for the course, and where the responsibility for both the quality and quantity of the experiences belonged to the students. Without the threat of grades and with the freedom to explore their own interests, I have found that students generally perform at a much higher level.*

*Without grades both my students and I felt freer
to interact together in a more open, honest, and
trusting relationship. The students felt much
freer to follow their own imagination, creativity
and uniqueness without the threat of failure.
Course outlines that used to be the road maps
to the grades became as flexible and tentative as
knowledge itself. My relationship with students
became much more personal, exciting, and
challenging. I knew my students as they really
were and not in roles they played in order to get
grades. With grades, we have fear, dependence,
and sameness. They toll a death knell for creativity, uniqueness, and open, honest trust.
Who is hurt most? For whom the grades toll I
cannot tell.[5]*

Alternative Two: Self-Grading for "B"

One way to avoid the risk of administrative pressure from
too many A's is to have mostly B's. Having nearly all C's or B's
rarely raises an eyebrow. This alternative is similar to the first
but modified slightly to produce mostly B's.

As in the first option, students have the responsibility to
grade themselves, but their choices are limited. Instead of having an A as the top grade, the top grade is a B. This is usually
accepted by most students when the reasons for self-grading
are explained. Those students who have secondary needs for
an A—such as parental pressure, honor society, or competition
for college admissions—can earn A's by doing an extra-credit
project agreed on by the student and teacher. The usual result
of this alternative is that most students get B's while a few get
A's. The teacher is using a self-grading system without being
too blatantly radical.

Obviously, this method does not give students as much of the responsibility for grading as does the first option, but the political and security gains make this option attractive in many situations when the first option is simply not feasible.

Alternative Three: Contract Grading

This method is similar to the first two. All the requirements for a given period of time are agreed on by the teacher and student and put in writing. Each party must have a say in the contract for this system to be effective. Contracts with no provision for student input are less effective because students see them as phony. Contracts with no provision for teacher input are equally ineffective. A contract that has both teacher and student input makes sure that students meet some minimum requirements that are important to the teacher while also allowing the students some freedom in pursuing their study.

One of the pitfalls of contract grading is that sometimes contracts become inflexible. Students might set unrealistic goals that are either too high or too low. One way to avoid this problem is to return the contracts to the students on a regular basis for revision.

Another potential problem is that students who use contracts tend to limit what they do to only what is written. This problem can be alleviated by having the teacher suggest several options for fulfilling the contract. A more difficult problem to resolve is faced by teachers who use a content-oriented approach. The content developed by students might not reflect the content desired. A compromise in terms of teaching style and allowable contract options must be worked out in this case.

The time span for contracts might differ with students of different ages. Younger students use shorter time frames, from a day up to a week. Very young students can use even hourly contracts. As students develop the ability to handle future commitments, the time span can increase to a week, a month, and finally, a term. I cannot provide you with a time-span/age chart. All students and classes are different, and you must make your own determination. You will be able to discover how effective your choices are through practice. If you are unsure, it is better to use shorter time frames and gradually increase them.

Successful contracts spell out the criteria for successful completion. They specify just what data or results will be used to indicate how well the criteria have been met. The data might be test results, a list of completed projects, descriptions of work, or a list of what the student has learned. Successful contracts also specify how the grade will be determined. The student, alone or in conjunction with the teacher, then determines the grade.

As with self-grading, one problem with contracts is that students might choose a grade that is either too high or too low. If you are worried about high grades, the contracts can be tied to a B with special provisions for A's.

Alternative Four: Peer Grading

Peer grading can be used in place of teacher grading in many instances. There are two possible ways to use this alterative effectively. The first method is to divide the class into groups of three to six and to have each group write a group contract. After completing the contract, the group can evaluate itself. Each student receives the group's grade. Groups can be formed according to the comfort students have in working with each other, or they can be organized around a mutual concern with a subject.

Peer grading is effective in a class with good group dynamics. It allows the weaker students to learn from their peers, which is often very effective when they are having trouble in traditional learning modes. Secondly, the students are often inspired by working with friends and peers on a common project.

However, a bad attitude by some students can drag down the rest of the group. If some students work harder than others, they will feel it is unfair to receive the same grade as those who worked less. This problem can be lessened by having each group determine its criteria for working together, while each student fills in the data aspect of the contract individually and receives an individual grade. This allows for perceived and real differences within the group. However, the group process and common bond that come from working for a group end is lessened.

The second method of peer grading is a variation of group work with an individual grade. In this alterative, the entire class, with teacher input, brainstorms the criteria for the contract. In effect, this is a total class contract. This method is especially useful for short-term learning assignments when it is best for the entire class to work on similar projects. This alternative might be less effective over long time frames, because the process would have to be repeated for each project.

Alternative Five: Blanket Grading

This alternative is designed to eliminate worry and concern over grading. Each student receives the same grade, usually an A or B, providing that some minimum standard is met. Those students who do not reach the specified standard must negotiate a grade individually with the teacher. For example, a teacher might give everyone in class a B. The minimum standard is reading X number of books, writing a paper, or filling in so many sets of small homework projects.

This alternative requires that an ongoing evaluation be part of regular class activities. Blanket grading could be harmful to students by simply declaring that everyone earns a B or A. Another problem is that most administrations are opposed to this concept, especially when the blanket grade is an A. Furthermore, the class as a whole might be unwilling to accept a blanket grade. This alternative must be explained thoroughly to administrators and students before going ahead with it.

SCHOOLWIDE CHANGES TO THE GRADING SYSTEM

It is extremely difficult for any one teacher to have a significant effect in reforming a school's grading policy. However, there are many options that can be adopted by schools or school systems that eliminate some of the potential hazards of traditional grading. But each of these alternatives has an inherent weakness. The following four alternatives are examples of the many grading alternatives available to schools.

Alternative One: Pass/Fail

Students meet established minimum standards, usually determined by the teacher. Meeting the standards results in a pass; not meeting them results in a fail. This alternative is the most widely used option in colleges and universities for courses that are not required. The basic advantages are that students have more leeway in determining procedures for meeting criteria and that artificial judgments are not imposed on students.

The disadvantages of this alternative are severe. First, many pass/fail systems do not specify clearly the criteria for success; the students are still caught in a guessing game of what is expected of them. Second, many teachers do not want to fail students and pass them regardless of whether or not they meet the stated criteria. Finally, the stigma of failure is still a part of this alternative; students are not allowed to experiment and fail without penalty.

Alternative Two: Credit/No Record

This option is an improvement over pass/fail because it eliminates the concept of failure. Students meet the minimum standard or receive no credit. They are not punished externally for not meeting the criteria. This system encourages students to try new subjects without fear. Younger students also benefit from this system, because they do not face the "failure" label.

Art Combs has compared this system to drivers' licensing. In order to receive a driver's license, an individual meets the standards set by the state and receives a certificate that gives one permission to drive. If an individual does not meet the standard (pass the driving test), no permission is given. There is no failure certificate issued nor is there a non-driver's license to follow them around for the rest of their lives. Credit/no record works in the same way.

The weaknesses in this system occur when the standards are not clearly specified to the students.

Alternative Three: Two-Track Grading

John Adams High School in Portland, Oregon, tried this alternative with success. Along with written evaluations four times a year, students in the school had a choice of grading systems. Those who wanted to be graded elected the "A-B-C/no record" track and were graded accordingly. Most of these students were college-bound students and took courses in which they felt they would be successful. This grading option had no failure attached. Other courses could be chosen on a "credit/no record" basis. The students could use either system for any course they elected. This system is a very effective alternative for secondary schools that want to change their grading system but have reservations about reporting to colleges.

Alternative Four: Performance Mastery

This system is derived from the performance-objectives approach to teaching. Objectives are specified either by the school or, in most cases, by the teacher; occasionally objectives can be specified by the students. Each objective that is met by a student is recorded, and the student receives credit. Instead of grades, a transcript lists the performances for which the student has demonstrated competence. The specificity and transferability of this system is attractive. One outgrowth of this approach has been the competency-based teacher education movement that was adopted in many states during the mid-1970s because of its ability to meet many of the purposes of grading.

This approach is not without inherent flaws. Performance mastery is a systems approach that has been adopted from industry; but because students are not products, the system has only limited use in a school context. It has been said of systems approaches that the system guarantees success; but if the wrong objectives are selected, a system will insure that the mistake is colossal.[5] Furthermore, only the most easily measurable, observable items are evaluated in this system. Creativity, values, feelings, and other difficult areas to measure are often left out. Still, this system provides a valid departure from traditional grading, as long as a more humanized, thorough, and personalized evaluation system is used concurrently.

These four alternatives are just examples of changes to a grading system that might be used as alternatives to a school's current system. A modification, blending, or a totally new alternative could be created to meet special circumstances. These alternatives are meant to be used exclusively as a recording system for keeping track of student progress within a closed system. As such, they take the place of grades. Alternatives beyond these are still needed to meet the other purposes for which grades are used.

Alternative Reporting Practices

Grades are also used for reporting to parents, screening, and reporting to future teachers, as well as for evaluating learning. Here are some alternative methods for meeting these needs.

REPORTING TO PARENTS

Each child is different, and all parents want different information, so one method of supplying appropriate information is to let each child's parents plan their own reporting system with the help of the teacher. This alternative has been tried with success in schools in Florida, New York, and California.

The first step is to have a teacher-parent conference in which the parents and teacher work out a format for reporting the child's progress. Suggested guidelines are: the information should be understood by parents, teachers, and students alike; the information should be reported in a reasonable amount of time; and all three parties must accept the format. Some parents want only short sentences, such as "Johnny is doing well in reading," "Mary has overcome a difficulty in math." Other parents want longer summaries in written form, usually a paragraph or two. Others elect a series of continua similar to grades.

This alternative has several advantages for the parents, such as closer contact between parents and teachers and the clarification of learning goals. There is more initial work on the teacher's part, and all teachers will need release time to establish a working process; but once the process is put into operation, it functions with little more work than is needed for traditional reporting.

One problem is that not all parents are willing to come to school and devise a reporting system. Usually, it is the parents whom teachers would like to see most who will not come to school. One school handled this problem by refusing to report any progress until contact was established. This brought in many, but not all, of the reluctant parents.

SCREENING

Information is used by college admissions officers and employers to screen applicants. Therefore, some system for supplying that information is needed. One suggestion is the portfolio system, which is currently used by art students who wish advanced schooling. Art students prepare a folder of their best work in the subjects required by the school. If the material meets the standards of the school, the student is accepted.

This system can be adapted for most screening purposes. Students who seek employment can provide information to demonstrate that they should be hired. Colleges can do the same as art schools: give a list of required and suggested areas for which students can indicate achievement. A potential English major could send poems, short stories, critical analyses of literature, and a bibliography of books read. Science majors could send lists of their experiments with one or two complete sets of lab notes, examples of creative problem-solving ability, a review of selected literature, etc. Admissions officers would distribute the portfolios to the appropriate departments for review by the staff.

INFORMATION FOR FUTURE TEACHERS

Teachers need information about students so that they are better prepared to meet each child's individual needs. Often, information passed from teacher to teacher has the opposite effect; one teacher's inaccurate impressions become a frame of reference for the next teacher. Some students never outlive the mistakes they made years earlier. Labels like "troublemaker," "slow," "bright," "stubborn," "lazy," or "poor home environment" are hard to outlive.

The teacher can do a better job by maintaining data concerning student work, including skill levels, development, and other significant information on what the child has accomplished. But gross generalizations and global judgments condemn students to a limited set of expectations. If a teacher sent the criteria for determining success and all the supporting data to the next teacher, this information would give the new teacher a more accurate view of the student.

---

1. Leeper, Robert, "For Whom the Grades Toll," unpublished paper, 1971.

2. Starch, Daniel, and Elliot, Edward, *School Review*, 1921, 20:442-445; 1913, 21:254-259.

3. Reynolds, Richard, *Los Angeles Times*, former high school teacher. Appeared in *Chicago Sun-Times*, 2 October 1966.

4. Ackerman, Paul, "The Effect of Honor Grading on Students' Test Scores," *American Educational Research Journal*, Vol. 8, No. 2, 1971: 330.

5. Wyatt, Susan, *The Mark: A Case for the Abolition of Grading*, (Washington, DC: Center for Educational Reform).

6. Leeper, Robert, "For Whom the Grades Toll," op. cit.

7. Combs, Art, Speech to the First National Conference on Grading Alternatives, Cleveland, Ohio, 1972.

Twelve

A Structure for Motivating the "Hard to Motivate"

Many people have written that instruction is a science. Some have argued that it is an art. Others have said it is a craft or intuitive skill. I am not completely sure. But this I know. When it is motivating, when there is a flow of learning and communication between instructor and learner, it is much more than all have written and said it was. It is a dimension, not something one practices or performs, but something one enters and lives.

— Raymond Wlodkowski
Enhancing Adult Motivation to Learn

I FIRST MET RAYMOND MANY YEARS AGO in New Orleans, where we co-taught an in-service course together. One of the most enjoyable experiences we shared was a jazz concert at the Preservation Jazz Hall. Sweet Emma Barrett was the featured pianist, a lady who must have been in her late seventies at that time. She suffered from arthritis and had to be wheeled up to the piano in a wheelchair. Even from where I was standing in the back of the hall, I could see the damage to her fingers. I still do not know where she found the dexterity to play the piano as masterfully and artfully as she did. Somehow the music transformed her, as if she had a new pair of hands. I hadn't asked for an autograph since I was in tenth grade, but on that night I bought a Sweet Emma Barrett record album in the lobby and asked her to autograph it. She held the pencil between two good fingers and etched a couple of letters on the jacket, and then she graciously shook my hand and thanked me for asking.

Raymond often says that teachers are advocates for what they teach.[1] Students look at them and intuitively ask, "What has it done for you?" If the answer is, "Not much," then students will not be attracted. Watching Sweet Emma Barrett exemplifies how people, even typically unmotivated children, are attracted by energy, by love for something they strongly believe in, and competence at what is important to them. They admire and respect those who are dedicated to performing in any arena, be it music, the arts, sports, or teaching. They are attracted to those who overcome obstacles graciously without whining or complaining of the difficulty. They respond positively to people with integrity and sincerity.

Motivation is more than what we say; it includes how we feel, what we value, what we do, and who we are. Motivation is intrinsically entwined with hope: hope inspires motivation and motivation inspires hope. Most dancers begin as youngsters. Rarely do performing dancers begin after the age of thirty. My sister, Joyce, began taking dancing lessons at an age when many dancers are past their prime, and within three years, she appeared in her first performance off Broadway. It was a student performance, showcasing the members of her class, but she was actually performing in New York City, and I was proud to be there to see her extraordinary dance performance. She never was able to explain her rare accomplishment except to say that she simply wanted to dance. Now she is taking acting lessons. It won't surprise me to see her perform in a play on Broadway someday. Some educators and psychologists consider hope and motivation to be the same. That is why this volume is as much about motivation as it is about hope. Whether or not this definition is literally accurate, it is true that hope inspires motivation and motivation leads to hope. This chapter will highlight some additional specific applications of motivation to classroom situations, especially for those at risk.

Students are motivated by many things in the classroom, including positive reinforcement, the desire to learn, the desire to please their teacher, the desire to please their parents, the desire to please their peers, the need to make a team or participate in an extracurricular activity, to eliminate or reduce failure, and to satisfy their natural sense of wonder. Unfortunately, most high risk students do not believe there is a reason to try. The traditional factors listed above rarely work with these students. Other avenues to encourage and motivate high risk students must be explored.

Positive reinforcement techniques, including rewards, tokens, and praise, have limited motivational value with most students because they focus on externals and do not touch the internal reasons why students do what they do. Also, there are many unintentional reinforcements in a classroom, so it is very difficult to control a schedule of reinforcement. In addition, rewards satiate; increasing amounts are required to produce the same effect. If you give a child a dollar to get an "A" in a first-grade subject, you will need many more to motivate the child by the time he is in high school.

Studies strongly indicate that when external reinforcement is used with naturally motivated students, they become motivated only by external rewards.[2] To paraphrase William Glasser, the fact is that motivation only comes from within the individual; the more the work that students are asked to do satisfies their needs, the harder they will work, and quality begets quality.[3]

For high risk students, reinforcement is even more problematic for two reasons. First, many students with a history of failure interpret praise and material rewards for successful experiences as pressure to continue to succeed. They believe that if they backslide, then they will be even greater failures. For example, a child who received mostly D's in math might become frightened that her parents will expect B's if she brings home a B+ on the mid-term examination. It is preferable for low-achieving students to stay where they are so that there is no threat of additional disappointment. The closer to the bottom, the smaller the fall. Second, for reinforcements to work, they must be desirable. Although some younger high risk students are motivated by smiley faces, candy, marbles in jars, or other gimmicks, these lose their appeal in a very short time.

PLEASING OTHERS

Some students try hard in school to please others: their parents, teachers, or peers. They are reinforced by the praise and positive regard they receive from these influential people. As with all positive reinforcers, the problem with pleasing others is that it focuses students on external goals. For students at risk, it is especially ineffective because their past experiences convince them that they will rarely please anyone through academic achievement. However, on those occasions when a teacher makes a special contact in a unique and personal manner with a high risk student, and when that teacher genuinely believes in the student, there is potential for successfully motivating the student in this way. Many students who finally succeeded after struggling in school credit their success to one teacher who cared and believed in them.

The most effective approaches to motivating high risk students are complex and encompass a variety of strategies, conditions, and classroom structures. The rest of this chapter will discuss 10 factors that can increase motivation. The more students feel or believe these factors, the greater their motivation will be.

1. *Students' motivation will increase when they accurately believe that they are competent in the subjects they are learning.*

Confidence in one's ability increases the desire to continue. Students who usually fail need more than just encouragement and inspiration. They need clear evidence that they can be successful because they are competent. Jack Frymier says that, "Those who are less motivated, less enthusiastic...feel that other people have the power; other people are in charge. These students feel fatalistic; moved by forces—benevolent or benign—but they do not feel responsible—able to respond— in the same way that those who are more positively motivated feel."[4]

I tried an interesting experiment with the class of "hard-to-motivate" students described in the preface, giving each student an A in every subject for the first grading period. I did this because I believed that telling my students that they could earn an A if they tried would be greeted with suspicion and cynicism. Teachers begin every year telling their classes that each student can be successful, and my students had heard it all before. I believed that once they received their A's, they would work to protect them.

I did not tell the students in advance what my plan was because I did not want to cheapen their accomplishments in their eyes. I told them after they received their first report cards that they had achieved all that was asked of them, and therefore they earned their grades. But I would be asking more of them next quarter.

There were three beneficial results to my experiment. The first two were unexpected. The students returned to class the day after they received their report cards with the same heart-warming story. They showed their grades to their grandparents who were so proud of them. It seemed to matter more that their grandparents were proud than their parents. Their joy in showing their cards to their grandparents moved me deeply. "Everyone," I thought, "deserves to feel their grandparents' pride in them at least once in their lives." I found it fascinating that the people they chose to please were their grandmothers. This was the first time I realized in a professional sense just how important multi-generation contact was for students who come from dysfunctional homes.

The second outcome was the statement I made to the building principal, who had written off both my students and me. He was furious that all my students made honor roll, top honors, in fact. "How can all of your students make honor roll when there are other, more capable students who learned more and didn't make it?" he asked accusingly. "My students did all that was asked of them," I responded. "What more can a student do? My students didn't take the place of anyone on the honor roll. There's plenty of room for any other student who belongs there."

The third and most important outcome was that, for the first time in their academic lives, my students had concrete evidence of success. They really did not earn their grades in the traditional sense. Their work and performance did not justify their grades by most academic standards. I do not advocate giving unearned grades. Simply telling students, even in an inspirational manner, that they can be successful if they try, will not motivate those students who have no history of successful school experiences. These students need tangible evidence that they have the ability to do what is asked of them. My students did a significant amount of work, without coaxing, during the next grading period.

My experiment is not meant as an example of how grades can be used as motivators. My experiment is an example of how one might manipulate the grading system (in ways not intended by the system) to change the perception of students who have been crippled by it. It is better to match the students' abilities to the tasks they are given, so that they can always be successful if they try. When complex tasks are too difficult, they can be broken down into their most basic steps. For example, during the second grading period, I developed a homework sheet with progressively difficult problems. The first night, the students had only to read the problems and write their names on the paper. The second night, they had to estimate answers to each problem without doing any computations. The third night, they had to do any three problems and compare their answers to their estimations. The sheet took over a week to finally complete. Each student achieved at a different level of difficulty. Subsequent math lessons were individualized for each student based on his mastery of the problems on the worksheet. Each student will be more motivated if he or she can competently achieve one learning goal or objective each day.

Teachers need to develop classroom activities in which all students can succeed. As difficult as this will be for teachers—and it requires a great deal of effort to start this process—it will be easier for teachers in the long run. First, once the system has been developed, it requires only modification, not new development, the next time around. Secondly, and more importantly, having students who do not try is more difficult than any curriculum development efforts. If at least some students improve, the work will be well worth it.

2. Student motivation will increase when school tasks are not too easy.

One of the dangers of giving students A's that they do not earn is that they may not value the achievement of any goal that they perceive as too easy. There is no pride in that. If we make school tasks too easy, students will see them as condescending and babyish. To take advantage of students' natural attraction to challenge, the challenge must be worth the effort.

The ideal tennis, racquetball, or bridge opponent is someone who is a little better than we are. If the opponent is not as good, we are not sufficiently challenged and become bored. If our opponent is much better, the frustration of trying to win is too great. When the opponent is just slightly better, we have to work hard to win; and when we do, it matters to us.

When taken together, factors one and two illustrate the need for individualized instruction. Classroom lessons are more motivating and successful when the challenges they offer students are matched to stretch their abilities. While most teachers love the concept of individualized instruction and understand its superiority, many are frightened by the amount of work involved in developing programs. But there are many commercial programs available that are quite good and save the teacher from starting from scratch. Other programs can be created without a great deal of development and still pay big motivational dividends.

One example of an easy-to-manage and inexpensive method for individualizing instruction was suggested to me by a colleague who taught seventh-grade English. Students wrote a paper once a week. The teacher identified just two errors in each paper, usually the ones made most frequently. Students wrote on an index card the name of the error and one example from their papers. When we studied grammar, each student took out one card and worked on learning how to correct it. We all studied grammar at the same time, but each student studied only what was relevant to him or her.

3. *Student motivation will increase when the topic is personally important and when what they are learning is congruent with their values.*

Abraham Maslow, in his book, *Eupsychian Management*,[5] says that for work to be rewarding and worth doing, it must fit in with the worker's value system. He gives an example of a man in a weapons factory. No matter how skilled he becomes at making weapons, he will never have pride in his work if he believes weapons are harmful.

Students, like workers, will take no pride in mastering a learning task that is inconsistent with their values. They will take pride in mastering those activities that are consistent with them. By taking the time to understand both the individual and cultural values of our students, we can make better choices of what material to present and how to present it.

High risk students often give the impression that they have few values and care about little except video games, television, and junk food. Both their behavior and attitudes often say clearly and loudly that they do not value anything related to school. I believe that the opposite is true, that they care deeply about school, but that they are afraid to take risks. When they say that they "could care less," they mean "to care is to hurt," and they are tired of feeling hurt.

When students have failed a class or are out of the mainstream of school activity, they are reluctant to share their values. The most opportune time to investigate your students' values is at the beginning of the year or the class, when they are less likely to have built up a protective wall. If the wall has already been built, it can be broken down by an active effort to treat all members of the class as equally important and welcome.

Teachers must be sensitive enough to not teach material that offends the values of their students. For example, presenting a balanced view of manifest destiny will help motivate Native Americans. The same holds true for Asian students when studying the internment of the Japanese during World War II. The Afrocentrism movement of the 1990s is rooted in the very real need for African-Americans to have their history and their versions of historical events be a legitimate part of the curriculum. Labeling single parent families, "Dysfunctional Families," is offensive to those who live in them. Celebrating only Christian holidays and using only Christian icons and symbols turns off non-Christian students.

Care can be taken in picking out which stories to read and how to interpret social, cultural, and historical events. We do not have to develop a new set of lessons for each group, but we can eliminate any material that is offensive to any group, especially if that lesson is based on single interpretations of complex phenomena.

By designing lessons and by using examples that are congruent with student values, teachers will provide a strong attraction for students to learn. For example, students who value counterculture might learn more about Shakespeare if they understood his father's countercultural stances and that he was fined for civil disobedience for not cleaning up the dung on the street outside his door. History is full of counterculture examples that might help students understand that freedom not only allows but requires an active countercultural movement for its survival.

Even those students who participate in gangs have a strong sense of values related to loyalty, bravery, and camaraderie. Gangs often serve the function of a family, and members share family-type values. A teacher studying the American family might look at the history of gangs as an example of a functioning alternative family. I am not suggesting that all courses become revolutionary or that teachers use artificial examples as window dressing to pull in the social outcasts. But there are many ways to include a variety of legitimate viewpoints that reflect alternative value systems. The arts, literature, music, history, social studies, current events, and science all encompass a cacophony of ideas, unusual characters, and events that can be used legitimately as the focus for instruction.

4. *Student motivation will increase when the student is actively involved in the learning process.*

The major single source of competition for your students' attention is television. Television is better than a teacher at keeping students passively watching, but it has inherent weaknesses that teachers can exploit. Televisions do not listen to children, do not challenge children, do not understand children, and especially do not allow children to do anything else while they are watching. The fact that children do so many other things while watching television suggests that television does not meet their needs for action and involvement.

A good example of how a hands-on curriculum can positively influence academic achievement is the creative arts approach of The Ashley River Creative Arts Elementary School in Charleston, South Carolina. Ashley River has become one of the top magnet schools by infusing the creative and performing arts into everyday school life. The principal, Rose Maree Myers, says that "The arts are a perfect means to diversify the curriculum, allowing a 'hands-on,' active approach to learning." In addition to specialized classes in visual arts, music, creative movement/gymnastics, and drama/creative writing, the arts are an integral part of every academic subject taught at the 585-pupil school.

In math, for example, a third-grader's introduction to fractions might begin with a session designing kaleidoscopes, and history might be paired with an art unit on the pottery skills of American Indians.[6]

There are many ways to involve students in the learning process, and all of them will help motivate the "hard to motivate" student. These include cooperative learning activities, games, mock elections or trials, role playing, acting out stories and plays, and allowing students to take over the role of teacher for part of the class.

An excellent example of involving students is the Diners' Club in a Bartlesville, Oklahoma, school. Jill Shackleford, the principal, and her staff developed the Diners' Club to help high risk students improve their behavior in the cafeteria and to involve them in the ongoing function of the school. In the club, students do not eat; they formally dine at tables especially dressed with tablecloths, place settings, and decorations. There are usually invited guests: parents, teachers, guest artists, or administrators. The students arrange everything, even the cleanup. When students graduate, they are qualified to receive a food handler's license. This exemplary program not only actively involves students, but it also gives them the message that they are competent and useful and that they matter. I visited the cafeteria when an EMH mainstreamed student was the lead manager of the club. As I watched these students perform at the weekly club luncheon, I would have guessed that only the best students in the school were running it. They behaved professionally and with great care, while they were having a lot of fun.

It is important to pay attention to the attention span of your students when they are involved in classroom activities. Because some activities are either too long or too short, students begin to act out or use their relative freedom to get into trouble. Activities are most effective when they have multiple entry and exit points, so that students can go on to something new or return to quiet seatwork when their attention span has worn out. Short attention spans may be gradually stretched; but when students are required to pay attention beyond what is natural, there will be problems.

Many teachers bemoan the short attention span of their students, but the problem is not limited to the classroom. Children learn by example. How long do we, as parents or teachers, listen to children before we say, "Hurry up, I have things to do"? How much attention do adults give to current events? We take in news as sound bites, not as stories. We read headlines, not lengthy articles. We want instant cures, not long-drawn-out treatments, for social problems. Teachers cover material, instead of investigating it in-depth. A school day is a quick tour through a number of subjects, rather than an in-depth treatment of any single subject. The source of short attention spans is our culture itself. School might be a place that offers an alternative, but we must accept the kind of children we have influenced as part of our own evolution.

Children of all ages love to move. They love to touch. They want to be heard. Let your students develop a dance as part of a lesson on geometry, or write and sing a song as part of a science lesson, and watch the tuned-out student come to life before your very eyes.

5. *Student motivation will increase when teachers demonstrate, in obvious ways, genuine energy and love of their subjects and for teaching.*

Dwight Allen, who was the Dean of the University of Massachusetts School of Education while I was there, exemplifies how love of teaching increases student motivation. Many years after he and I were no longer in Amherst, I met him on a plane. I asked him what he was doing and he told me this story:

> *I am currently a professor emeritus at old Dominion University in Virginia. You know that I think in symbols, and I wanted to make a point about motivation, so I polled a great number of students and asked them what the worst and most hated course was. I then asked a number of professors what course was the least favorite to teach. The same course topped both lists—freshman composition. I told the administration not only that I wanted to teach the course, but I promised that students could be highly motivated by the course. That would prove that any course can be motivating, and no one could truthfully say that students cannot be motivated to learn.*

> *Within two years, my section of freshman composition was one of the most popular courses at the university. My approach was to use as a text, a book with no words, Anno's Journey.[7] Anno is a Japanese painter who illustrated the cultural*

history of Europe in what is mostly regarded as a children's book. It is filled with visual humor, time shifts, and a complex story line based on illustrations, not words. I developed a study guide for the course that asked students to ponder questions such as: How are stories told? Can there be puns in a book with no words? How is humor created? Can there be a chronology in a book with no words? How is irony demonstrated in this book? What is the difference between a written and a visual metaphor? The intrigue of learning to write from a book with no words was enchanting enough to generate a high level of motivation in my students.

More than anything else, what made the course enchanting was Dwight's love of teaching and his commitment to motivating his students.

It is compelling to pay attention to those who love what they do. I remember watching a most unusual jazz concert at The Great America Music Hall in San Francisco. Drummer Freddie Hutcherson finally arrived, but his drums were still in transit. "No problem," he said loudly enough for the audience to hear him, "I'll just play this chair." For the next set, he played a chair borrowed from the audience as if it were a new style drum, experimenting with various sounds he could create. His wide grin and his energy showed us all how much he enjoyed the challenge and the thrill of discovery. The drums arrived for the next set, but Freddie didn't want them. "I haven't mastered the chair yet," he explained. "Just give me the cymbals. I might want to use a chair in my next album."

There is a great natural attraction to people who love what they do, be it on the stage or screen, at the ball park, or in the concert hall. Genuine, unrestrained passion commands our attention and makes us care. This is true even in the classroom.

Recall your favorite teachers. Most of them loved what they taught. You got caught up in their energy, and you could not help being caught up in it. You can provide the same inspiration for your students by following these suggestions:

- Remember why you wanted to be a teacher. Keep those reasons in mind every day you teach.

- Understand what you love to teach and what you do not. Teach more of what you love and find ways to energize yourself for what you don't by using techniques and methods you enjoy, or by teaching it in a way that the kids enjoy.

- Do at least one activity you love at least once a day, or once a period for secondary teachers. The special activity might only take five minutes of class time. Focus on how much you are looking forward to teaching it on your way to school.

- Ignore cynical teachers or administrators. Do not let them diminish your love of teaching.

- Strive to be a great teacher every day. Take pride in your profession and your ability to do it well. Think of yourself as the Bruce Springsteen, Barbra Streisand, Frank Sinatra, or Joe Montana of teaching.

- Do not be afraid to show off. Let yourself go, and be a ham every now and then for your students.

- Let your students know why you love teaching, and why you love what you teach. Do this with energy and commitment, not preaching.

• Do the unexpected; surprise your students and surprise yourself. Make your classroom an event. Look forward to being there and do things that get your students to think, "I wonder what will happen next," rather than, "I wonder if I can make it through another class?"

6. Student motivation will increase when students perceive that classroom activities and goals are real, not just gimmicks.

There is nothing wrong with using clever gimmicks to spice up a lesson to capture students' attention. A good gimmick can provide the showmanship to compete with all the flashy stimuli in our students' lives, such as television and music. Many motivational suggestions focus on flashy ways to dress up lessons in the same way that advertisements are dressed up to catch the consumer.

However, gimmicks cannot sustain the attention of students unless they connect with the basic needs of students. Students with real learning difficulties will be attracted initially to the flash; but if they perceive the gimmick as phony, they will not value the lesson. They may pay attention, possibly to relieve the boredom of being in school, but that does not mean they will learn. Jack Frymier writes:

> *Meaningfulness is the extent to which that which is perceived makes sense or is seen as significant or potentially useful to the student....meaningfulness is a personal matter. It is affected by one's previous experiences and personal values and a sense of adequacy. Unless the student is able to see some personal relevance or potential usefulness for the information, it is not meaningful, thus not of interest.*[8]

The surest way to sustain learning after the attraction of the flash wears off is to ensure that what students learn will be beneficial to them, both in the immediate and in the long-term future. In addition, the material *must be perceived as beneficial by the students.* Developing lessons that are intrinsically motivational takes more time and more planning than developing flashy ones, but they are worth it. Even better are meaningful lessons with enough flash to capture the students' attention and enough substance to sustain it over time.

7. Student motivation will increase when the lessons are fun and enjoyable.

Fun is motivating. Enjoyment is attractive. These two concepts are not revolutionary, except when they are mentioned in school. Imagine a reluctant student in your class who refuses to do anything. If he sits there while other students are having fun, there is a strong likelihood that he will ask to join in. When learning is fun, the students will be more motivated and will remember the lessons much longer.

Learning is not always fun, and students often can learn from unenjoyable tasks. We do not have to sugarcoat every school task. However, just because we cannot make all lessons enjoyable does not mean we should try to make them repulsive. There is an element of enjoyment even in rigorous learning activities when they are planned that way.

With marginal students, we need all the attraction we can get. There should be an element of fun built into each lesson or activity. Every student will benefit, and the teacher also will enjoy it more.

8. Student motivation will increase when students feel welcome in school and in their classrooms, when they feel that they belong in school.

This topic was discussed in Chapter 3, but it bears repeating. If the student believes that school is a hostile environment, then doing what the school wants is giving in to the enemy. Even individualized, useful, and fun lessons will never be tried by students who are unwilling to try. Somehow, they must be encouraged to enter into an activity. A positive attitude will encourage students to take the risks necessary to begin mastery of a new topic or skill.

Students should be guaranteed that they will never be embarrassed for giving wrong answers or not knowing something. Their learning struggles should be kept private. This does not mean that teachers should not call on them; call on them as often as you call on the better students. But maintain their dignity when they either cannot or will not answer.

When they know from what you do, as well as what you say, that they are welcome members of the class, regardless of what they do, you will increase your chance to motivate them.

9. Student motivation will increase when a teacher makes a personal connection to the student.

Even the students who are most isolated in school have a teacher who makes a difference to them. These are teachers who have gone out of their way to make personal contact in a meaningful way. Greet students personally every day. Teachers can show a personal interest in students by asking them questions about their lives and by engaging in discussions with them about things other than academics. These discussions can be brief; it is more important to engage students regularly over time than to have a long talk once or twice a year.

In *Discipline with Dignity*, Al Mendler and I describe a strategy called "adopt a friend,"[9] to help disabled students in regular classroom settings. The same technique can be used for high risk students. It is based on the concept of mentoring. Each targeted student is "adopted" by a willing and able teacher. This teacher seeks out the identified student informally and makes a strong, positive connection.

When there is a caring, positive role model in the school for those students on the edge, there is a greater likelihood that they will respond to other motivational techniques. Someone who takes pride in them when they succeed and encourages them when they fail might be the most important influence in their lives. For those students with little or no positive contact with their parents, a school mentor might make all the difference in the world.

10. Student motivation will increase when teachers pay attention to motivation and plan for it.

Motivation does not magically appear. It requires attention and planning. It is too important to simply assume you will get it if your lessons are worthwhile. Remember that your "hard to motivate" students have experienced "worthwhile" lessons for the entire time they have been in school. If they still are not motivated, then they need something else. By your giving it to them, at least some of them might find the joy in learning that will overcome negative thinking about school.

---

1. For additional information about motivating students to learn see Wlodkowski, Raymond, *Motivation and Teaching*, NEA, Washington, D.C., 1978; and Wlodkowski, Raymond, and Jarnes, Judith, *Eager to Learn* (Jossey-Bass, San Francisco, 1990).

2. Curwin, Richard, "Are Your Students Addicted to Praise?" *Instructor* 90, 3 (1980):61-62.

3. Malouf, David, "Do Rewards Reduce Student Motivation?" *School Psychology Review*, 12, no. 1 (1983):

4. Glasser, William, "The Quality School," *Phi Delta Kappan* 71 (1990):427.

5. Frymier, Jack, *Motivation to Learn*, Phi Delta Kappa, Bloomington, 1985. p. 13-14.

6. Csikszentmihalyi, Mihay, *Flow* (Harper and Row, 1990) p. 2.

7. Ibid., p. 64.

8. Ibid., p. 75.

9. Maslow, Abraham, *Eupsychian Management: A Journal* (Homewood, Illinois: Irwin-Dorsey, 1965).

10. Greenfield, Meg, "The War Keeps Going and Going," *Newsweek* (15 April 1991):80.

11. Healy, Michelle, "South Carolina School Makes Crafts Part of the Lesson Plan," *USA Today* (17 April 1991):7A.

12. Anno, Mitsumasa, *Anno's Journey* (New York: Philomel Books, 1977).

13. Frymier, op. cit., p. 13-14.

14. Wlodkowski, Raymond, *Motivation and Teaching*, Washington, DC: NEA, 1978).

15. Curwin, Richard, and Mendler, Allen, *Discipline With Dignity* (Washington, DC: ASCD, 1988), pp. 190-191.

Thirteen

School Policies and Practices

Nothing will ever be attempted if all possible objections must first be overcome.

— Samuel Johnson

What on earth would a man do with himself if something did not stand in his way?

— H. G. Wells

S CHOOL POLICIES SEND STRONG MESSAGES to administrators, teachers, and especially students. Policies reflect the values of the school. They set the tone for the entire school and tell students how important they are in the total scheme of things. If the policies are designed to protect the school from the students, then they will define the battle lines for those children who experience school negatively. On the other hand, if the policies protect the students, they will allow the school to connect with those students.

Many policies seem to exist only because they have always existed and are deeply entrenched. Other policies reflect careful consideration by those who created them and of those who carry them out. Regardless of how a policy was created, we can measure all of them by the following standard: based on hope, are they in the best interest of children, especially those at risk.

Sometimes school policies act as an accelerator. They promote new procedures and techniques to better meet the goals of the school. For example, the policy of improving students' performance might encourage the addition of cooperative learning and critical thinking skills to the curriculum. The principal might invoke school policy to encourage a foot-dragging teacher to try something new.

Sometimes school policies act as a brake. They give administrators an excuse to prevent teachers from trying new things. For example, a teacher might wish to experiment with a new grading system. The principal can cite school policy to prevent such experimentation.

Dwight Allen had this to say about educational innovation and school policies.

> *If I want to change a school policy or implement
> an innovation and you ask me to prove that what
> I want to do will work, then show me the proof
> that what you are now doing works. I will match
> your proof. If you have strong evidence that what
> you are currently doing is making a positive dif-
> ference, then I better have even more evidence
> that my innovation will improve the school. But
> if you don't have any evidence at all, then get out
> of my way and let me have a chance.*

Unfortunately, the burden of proof always rests with the change agent and never with the establishment, even though the establishment might have no evidence whatsoever that the existing system makes any sense. The grading system described in Chapter 11 is an example. There is no evidence that it is helpful to students, and there is significant evidence indicating that it is harmful; yet it still continues to exist in most schools. No one has figured out how to get rid of it.

The most common school policies that affect students are related to such issues as retention, tracking, suspension and expulsion, testing, and the honor roll. Many people believe that the only legitimate answer to all of these issues is to completely redesign the structure of schools in a way that makes each of these policies obsolete. As hopeful as I am that schools can change, I have little hope that we will redesign schools in this manner, at least on a large scale. There are a number of schools, mostly private, that have built their policies from scratch and redefine what a school can be. However, for most educators the most realistic approach is to take what we have and work to make it better.

Some of the more cynical will say that the chance of changing even a fragment of school policy is as remote as that of changing our entire education system; it will not happen. I disagree. There are too many teachers, principals, and even superintendents who have the energy and commitment to change schools for the better. Change might seem slow, but we can never let the system control education. The system must always be a tool, not a master, for doing whatever is necessary for children to learn.

The following questions can be used as a guide to help determine if your policies are effective for helping high risk students to be hopeful students in your school:

1. *Are school policies designed for protection or growth?*

It is time to stop setting school policies from a defensive position and to start determining our own destiny. Educators need the courage to establish policies that improve education for students instead of policies that protect educators from all the critics, complainers, and others who have their own agendas for what happens in schools.

2. Are there any policies that interfere with student learning?

A policy that is designed to make the school run more efficiently but which interferes with student learning actually makes the school less efficient in the long run. An example is a grading system that helps evaluate students efficiently but does not promote an increase in the students' desire to learn.

3. Are there any policies that protect the school rather than all students?

School policies are designed for protection. They guide administrators and teachers when they make decisions. Sometimes the policies sacrifice the needs of the students for the needs of the system. System approaches work both for and against the high risk student. When the system is designed to protect the student, it elicits a favorable response from the student. When the rules protect the organization, they alienate the student. Imagine your feelings when you call an airline or a major credit card company only to be greeted by a voice-mail menu of options. None of the options really apply to your problem, but you select the closest choice. You are greeted by another menu, then you must listen to a number of selected messages. Finally, you are given another number to call, followed by a busy signal. There is no option that meets your particular need.

Students feel the same way about school. When they are put off by an efficient but impersonal system, they react with anger and frustration, not appreciation.

An example of a bad policy is one that gives all students detention for being late after lunch, even though it takes the students at the end of the food line longer to get their food than the time they are allotted to eat.

4. Do school policies treat all students the same, or do they treat each student as an individual with individual needs?

The dangers of treating every student the same has been previously explained. Check your policies to see if they allow sufficient flexibility to make individual choices for treating individual children.

There are educators who believe that because some teachers and administrators will abuse this principle, students need protection. Their answer is to treat everyone the same to ensure fairness. All students need to be treated fairly, but policies that treat all students the same never protect anyone. If a teacher or administrator is out to get a student, then a policy will not save that student. The protection of students depends on professionalism and good will, not policy.

5. Are there specific provisions built into your daily school rituals to ensure that every student feels welcome every day?

Is each student in your school personally greeted each morning by a teacher or administrator? Does something happen in the school to tell each and every student that you are glad that they are there? Or is the focus on getting them to conform? Do the school rituals pit students and teachers against each other, or do they bond them together to work for mutual goals?

6. Do school policies ensure that all students, regardless of their cultural background, sex, and individual characteristics are treated without prejudgment or condescending, limiting expectations?

7. Do the policies provide training and coaching for those teachers who lack the awareness, skill, and knowledge to reach high risk students?

Many teachers have not had the necessary training to deal effectively with the most troubled students in school. Most university courses do nothing, or very little, to train preservice teachers for the reality of the high risk student, so providing that training is left to inservice programs.

Inservice training should provide both encouragement and skills. One without the other is insufficient. Platitudes and encouragement will do little to help without teaching the faculty the skills they need to do the job.

Refresher courses and continued training should be an ongoing and regular part of school life. Schools are a place of learning for all who are there. When learning is valued by the administration and faculty as something they believe in and do, they are stronger advocates for learning for their students. When staff are unwilling to learn, or when the school does not provide ongoing learning activities as a regular part of the job, the value of learning becomes empty words, not visible to students as part of reality. Schools have the best chance to reach all students when teachers are continually learning and when ongoing instructional activities for teachers and administrators are a regular part of the school year. These schools say by what they do that they value learning.

No one questions the need for building and grounds maintenance. People maintenance is just as important. Training faculty and staff is a critical function of an effective school, especially because students are constantly changing.

8. *Do policies label students, especially those at risk?*

When labels are substituted for understanding, serious errors are committed. It is easy to label and hard to understand the complex reasons for why children do what they do.

The above questions can be applied to each policy in your school. Revising bad policies will work best when administrators and teachers work together to determine which are the most effective. If there is disagreement about whether or not a policy should be modified or removed, ask each of these questions.

a) Who does the policy help most? Who will a new policy help?

b) Does the old policy promote or hinder learning?

c) Does the policy promote or hinder individualized treatment of students?

d) Does the policy treat students with dignity? Does it make all students feel welcome in school?

e) How does the policy help the angry, low achieving, alienated high risk student become hopeful about being in school?

Let us examine some specific school policy issues that are common to all schools.

HOMOGENEOUS GROUPING

There are many reasons given for the use of ability groups. It is unfair for students of different abilities to compete against each other. It is too difficult for teachers to prepare for classes with wide variances of ability. Ability grouping is just another form of individualized instruction, but on a larger scale. Ability groups provide hope for the high risk student by keeping the competition and material at a level designed for success. A study by Jomills Henry Braddock found that when used wisely, instructional grouping strategies help schools meet the varying needs of students and create a positive learning environment in schools.[1]

There are many reasons why ability grouping hurts students, especially those at risk. Ability grouping is simply another form of discrimination. Ability grouping sacrifices what is best for students for what is most efficient. Ability grouping predetermines student expectations; lower groups achieve lower results. Tracking reduces exposure to different levels of thought and behavior. Tracking reduces hope by limiting the potential of the high risk student. A study of nearly 11,000 students, published in 1989, calculated that those who were in the slowest track were more likely to drop out as a result of being in that track.[2]

With such strong arguments on both sides, it is hard to make sense of the tracking debate.

In high school, I was an advanced placement English student. For two years, I studied college level literature and wrote college level essays. I loved English and behaved maturely during my English classes. My teacher, Miss Bussey, told me before I signed up for the class that my test scores were lower than those of the other students, but my desire was higher, and with effort I could be successful. During a tearful reunion fifteen years after my graduation, she told me I was the only writing student she ever taught who actually published a book.

Because I never seemed to be able to master foreign languages, I took basic French. French for shop majors is what we called it. In French class, the teacher treated me like a jerk. I was always in trouble for pulling girls' hair, throwing spitballs, talking back, not doing homework, and behaving like a baby. I never saw my French teacher again, and now the only French words I know are "Filet Mignon."

In this case, tracking definitely established my own expectations both for behavior and for academic success. Because my English teacher believed in me, I was challenged, rather than frightened, by work that was supposedly over my head.

If I had been placed in advanced placement English and told, "Your test scores are lower than other students in this class. You will never do as well as them," and I heard the first time I scored poorly on a test, "See, I told you, you weren't that good," I would have given up.

I wanted to do well in English because I loved it. I predicted from the time I was young that someday I would be a writer. I loved reading and read every book I could get my hands on.

The same could not be said of French. All the encouragement in the world would not have led to a successful experience for me. I had no hope for success nor any reason to do well. My skills were poor and my desire matched my skills.

When I look at tracking, I see many students who have shared experiences such as mine. It is very difficult to understand whether tracking improves hope or destroys it for those students at risk. Anne Lewis cites the persistence of tracking as the source of many of the constraints hindering efforts to create a better educational system.[3] The Braddock study mentioned above also points out that when tracking is used unwisely, it exaggerates differences, labels some students as slow or stupid, and results in a poor climate for learning.

The question is: How can tracking be used wisely? I suggest the following for tracking to be successful:

1. *Make tracking voluntary.* Allow students to select the best track for themselves. If a student wants to participate at a higher or lower level than his scores indicate, allow him to try it his way. To help the student make the best decision, provide counseling that lets him or her know what the expectation will

be at each level. Let students know what their skills are. Also let them know that skills and expectations do not always form an equation. Counseling should always be designed to help the child make a wise decision, not to limit his potential or to push him beyond his comfort level. The decision should be in the best interests of the child, not those of the teacher or school.

It also might help if each teacher could make presentations about their courses and their requirements to the entire student body at the beginning of each term to give the students a sampling of their options. These presentations could be offered in the form of an education fair, which would be fun for the faculty and students and would add an element of excitement to the beginning of the year. When I taught at San Francisco State in the Secondary Education Department, all of the seminar teachers did something like this at the beginning of the year, and it was a wonderful opportunity for faculty and students alike.

2. *Make tracking fluid.* Allow students to move between tracks during the year, so that students who realize that they made a mistake can move up or down until they find the best level. This strategy works best when individualized instruction is a regular part of the learning process.

Various tracking levels are not substitutes for individualized learning opportunities. Teachers need training in how to deal with a changing roster, with students moving up and down the sequence during the year. Fluidity will work best if it has few restrictions, but it will be more efficient if there are pre-established entry and exit points, perhaps at the beginning of each quarter.

3. *Eliminate competition between students and build cooperative classroom environments.* In Chapter 11, I discussed how

the grading system can be modified. Those modifications are most helpful in making a free-choice tracking system work. When non-competitive grading systems are combined with non-competitive classroom activities (Chapter 10), there will be no need to worry about whether a high risk student is competing unfairly with other students who may be achieving at a higher level.

When students are involved in shared instructional activities, including cooperative learning strategies, they help and teach each other. Peer teaching is not only helpful to the student on the receiving end, it also immeasurably helps the student who is teaching. When the student at risk is helped by the other students rather than being placed in competion with them, social benefits also result. Students feel less isolated and more in the mainstream of school life.

4. *Introduce more interdisciplinary and thematic courses for students to choose in the tracking system.* Interdisciplinary courses will increase student chances for success by allowing skills in one area to be useful in other areas. Students with high verbal skills but who are less skilled in science, can be successful in projects that include writing or orally reporting about science. As part of a team, the student with high verbal skills can help the student skilled in science and both will benefit.

These suggestions will drastically change the nature of tracking. In addition to altering the manner in which students are placed, they will alter the way in which instruction is organized and delivered. These suggestions will obviously benefit the lower-achieving students by increasing opportunities without increasing negative competition. Hope will always exist, and the dignity of the student will always be maintained. The higher-achieving students will also benefit by these suggestions.

RETENTION

Because students at risk are the most likely to be retained, it is important that retention benefits students by improving their ability to learn, by increasing their motivation to learn, and by increasing their hopefulness about school. Shepard and Smith estimate that 5% to 7%, or about two children in every classroom, are retained in the United States annually.[4]

However, the research clearly indicates that keeping a child back a grade does not work. Shepard and Smith's review of the research on grade retention points out that:

1. Retained children actually perform more poorly on average when they go to the next grade than if they had been promoted without repeating a grade.

2. Dropouts are five times more likely to have repeated a grade than high school graduates.

3. The annual cost to school districts of retaining 2.4 million students per year is nearly $10 billion.

With such strong evidence against retention and such a dearth of evidence in its favor, why are students still being retained? There may be some cases where retention can be helpful; for example, when children are both physically and emotionally more immature than other students in their grade and when the students themselves prefer it. My son, Danny, was retained—a decision into which I had virtually no input, although I agreed to be the one to inform him. I procrastinated the dreaded task of telling him for about three weeks. I worked out an explanation focusing on as many positive aspects of the decision as possible, but when I started to go into it with him, he was so relieved and positive about it that my long explanation was unnecessary. Because he saw the retention as an opportunity, and because he was very bright, but immature for his age, he actually benefited greatly from the experience.

Maybe there are other students who likewise can benefit, but the decision must always be made with considerable caution. If, as one critic charges, the major reason retention is still used is that "schools are under considerable pressure to maintain acceptably high levels of grade retention as proof of high standards,"[5] then there is nothing courageous about retaining students. The negative effects on most students who are retained are too severe to be decided in this manner.

Teachers can help reduce the number of retentions by individualizing their instruction to accommodate various levels of learning. Administrators can establish a multitude of programs to eliminate the need for retention. There are several other options to help those students who might be held back a grade. These alternatives can be set up at both the school and classroom level. Shepard and Smith suggest:

- Remedial help

- Before- and after-school programs

- Summer school

- Instructional aides working with target children in the regular classroom

- Peer tutoring

- The use of individualized instructional plans

- Special staffing sessions with teachers from the current and next year to develop programs to meet students' needs

When schools make changes in the system, the need for retention may well disappear.

HONOR ROLL

Honor rolls are used to honor the best students. Advocates say that schools should honor more than athletics, and that honor rolls are like an all-star list for high academic achievement. Honor rolls are often published in newspapers and posted in the front hallways of schools. Local restaurants even offer kids on the honor roll free food. Honor rolls lead to graduation with honors and other academic distinctions.

I can hear the protests of honor-roll parents now, but I think it's time to eliminate or minimize this practice. Learning is not sports, and there can be no joy in the winners of the academic game without equal tears for the losers. Because school, unlike sports, is involuntary and exists equally for all students, we need to minimize the trappings of a caste system that has no academic benefits.

Furthermore, honor rolls help promote an attitude of "what's in it for me?" Rather than have an honor roll that promotes self-centeredness, maybe it's time for an honor roll for the students who do the most for the community. Or maybe an honor roll for those who try the hardest. A "D student" who goes to a C makes it, but an "A student" who does not bother to try does not.

The top students know who they are and don't need the honor roll to motivate them. They can be acknowledged by other means—allowing them to tutor and help the less gifted, for example. Policy that segregates low achieving students from the high achievers and says that some students are more welcome than others in school is more a hindrance than a help.

The odds are that change will be slow, because honor rolls are firmly entrenched and have the blessing of apple pie and motherhood. However, teachers can set up their own alternative honor rolls that honor effort. That may prevent borderline students from becoming hopeless and reclaim those that already are.

CLASS SIZE

Teachers do not determine class size. Neither do building administrators. Often, superintendents have little say in the matter. The usual determiner of class size is available resources. Without money, there are few options. The research on class size indicates that class size affects students more in elementary school than in the higher grades, and that increases in class size affect high risk students more than other students.

The obvious reason that increased class size affects students at risk is because it limits the amount of attention they receive. The more students in a class, the more students who can fall between the cracks. When teachers do not have the time to attend to the special needs of high risk students, the students' performances may worsen and behavior problems may increase. If teachers shift priorities and give high risk students the attention they need, other students may suffer. The result may be more students developing "high risk" symptoms.

Teachers and administrators cannot do much about the size of different classes at any given time, but as a group, all educators can mobilize and make their needs known to those who control the budget. Ultimately, it will be in the best interest of everybody for schools to educate taxpayers about the costs of increasing class size.

SUSPENSIONS AND EXPULSIONS

In-school suspension can be an effective tool if the time spent during the suspension period is used to help students learn new skills for improving their behavior. Simply removing a student from class may provide temporary relief for both the student and the teacher, but it will do little to resolve the problem when the student returns to class.

Sometimes the teachers who supervise the in-school suspension room can offer more individualized attention, because there is a smaller number of students and because they have no responsibility to cover a prescribed amount of material. If there are students who thrive on in-school suspension and prefer to be there, they might be in need of additional support services to be successful in the regular classroom.

Out-of-school suspension should be used only as a last resort for those students too violent or volatile to stay in school. Years ago, a suspended child went home to a parent or supervising adult. But times have changed; today, children are typically unsupervised at home. There is little chance that any educational goals, either academic or behavioral, can be achieved. When students return to school, the only changes are stronger feelings of anger, revenge, and alienation. They are prime candidates for future confrontations.

The expulsion option is rarely used. Rather than permanently remove worst-case students from school, more can be gained by placing them in alternative educational programs and schools designed to meet the needs of non-mainstream students. When alternative schools are structured to help alternative kids, they offer genuine successful experiences.

Administrators can help by providing in-school suspension rooms in every school. However, establishing such a room is not enough. Training for faculty in how to use the concept of in-school suspension is as important as the room itself. Teachers should not think of the room as a dumping ground for their problems; suspension rooms are places for children to cool down and develop plans before returning to class.

Teachers can help by learning the most effective ways to use the suspension option to help their students learn responsibility. It obviously helps the other students as well as the teacher to remove an explosive child; but removal only postpones the educational part of the solution. Students must still learn how to become responsible,

STANDARDIZED TESTING

President Bush has called for a national test of student achievement. Governor Wilson of California recently signed into law a plan for a statewide test of all students. It would seem that standardized tests are becoming a permanent fixture of American education.

Whether the rebirth of the testing craze will improve or worsen education depends on how test scores are used, and on who uses them. At one time, standardized tests were used to measure how well students were learning, and they served this task fairly well.

Chris Pipho points out the relationship between instruction and assessment, where one end of the continuum is "teaching to the test," and the other leads more toward legitimate curricular and instructional change.

> *The politics of testing, due to the demands for accountability, have strong implications for what we teach and how we teach it. The stakes are high, and the result, unfortunately, has been disaster. As George Madaus says, "When the stakes are high, people are going to find ways to have test scores go up....If it's important enough, people are going to find ways to get kids over the hurdle of the tests. The school will look better, but the skill levels will not necessarily be going*

*up. You may have succeeded only in corrupting
the inferences you want to make from the tests.*"[6]

Deming says that production increases by eliminating numerical quotas. When this principle is applied to testing, Alan Blankstein says that:

*Setting quotas leads to marginal work. If a
teacher is evaluated on how many of her students
receive a passing grade of 60%, then she will
strive to have as many as possible do just that.
She will not be as inclined to help those who are
way below or well above that mark, or move
everyone toward excellence. This leads to the
"finish Mao Tse-Tung by Friday" syndrome
(Sizer, 1991), in which mastery is not the goal.*[7]

There are two specific dangers of standardized testing that affect high risk students. The first is that if tests determine curriculum rather than the other way around, the amount of flexibility that teachers have to modify instruction to meet the specific needs of high risk students will be sharply reduced. The majority of those who have investigated the effects of testing believe this is happening and will increase in the future. Samuel Meisels says that:

*This phenomenon, known as "measurement-dri-
ven instruction" (Madaus 1988), transforms testing programs, ideally servants of educational
programs, into masters of the educational
process. The results are a narrowing of the curriculum, a concentration on those skills most
amenable to testing, a constraint on the creativity and flexibility of teachers, and a demeaning of
teachers' professionals judgment.*

Neill and Medina maintain that standardized testing often results in teaching that is coaching for the test. In too many schools, real learning and real thinking are crowded out.[8]

The second danger to high risk students is that standardized tests limit which skills are important, ignore important areas in which marginal students might be successful but which are hard to test, and lead to pressure to conform to a single standard of success. The more standardized testing is used to determine which schools and teachers are successful, the greater the wedge driven between the goals of instruction and the educational needs of high risk students. Marginal students will give up trying because they will perceive (and rightly so) that the system is being used against them.

Everyone who works with children must work actively to prevent the current testing movement from destroying the hope of children. We do not need to eliminate standardized testing, but we must control how these tests are used. We must be diligent in making sure that tests never drive the curriculum and that students do not suffer by their use. We can use the information they produce diagnostically to develop better teaching strategies and individualized programs.

Administrators can help by minimizing the importance given to tests that cannot be eliminated. In faculty meetings and individual conferences, training can show how to use tests diagnostically rather than judgmentally. Administrators can go a long way toward reducing testing phobia among staff and students.

Teachers must refuse to teach to the test. The decision of what to include in the curriculum should never be based on what is in the test, but rather on what is most important for students to learn. The focus of learning is best placed on understanding and using information, not the information itself. Everyone can remember that it makes no difference what we teach or what the tests show; all that matters is what students learn.

SCHOOL WITHIN A SCHOOL

Schools do not set out to turn students off, but they are often so large and impersonal that they do it anyway. One way to cut down on the impersonal nature of a large school is to create a school within a school. By creating a school within a school, the numbers are reduced and students feel that they matter. Fewer students fall through the cracks. The high risk students can be given more individual attention by both teachers and administrators.

Teachers and administrators can work together to create a school within a school. Once the concept is accepted, a decision must be reached on the theme of the school. Will it be based on academics or interest? Will it be based on grades? Will it be a cross-section of every grade? The school within a school may have its own student government and its own administration and faculty. Once the theme is decided, the hard work of developing programs begins.

The above policy suggestions, if implemented, will help to establish a school where student learning is the highest value. They will increase the chances that students at risk will feel welcome in school and that they will feel more hopeful about their chances for success.

---

1. Braddock, Jomills Henry II, "Tracking the Middle Grades: National patterns of Grouping for Instruction," *Phi Delta Kappan* 71 (1990):445-49.

2. Cohn, Alfie, "Tracking Derailed," *Parenting Magazine* (September 1990):40.

3. Lewis, Anne, "Washington Commentary: Tracking and the National Goals," *Phi Delta Kappan* 72 (1990):100-101.

4. Shepard, Lorrie, and Smith, Mary Lee, "Synthesis of Research on Grade Retention," *Educational Leadership* (May 1990):84.

5. Ibid., 88.

6. Pipho, Chris, "Stateline: The Uses of Test Scores," *Phi Delta Kappan* 70 (December 1988): 278-79.

7. Blankstein, Alan, "Lessons from Enlightened Corporations," *Educational Leadership* 49, 6 (1992): 71-75.

8. Meisels, Samuel, *Educational Leadership* (April 1989): 17

Fourteen

Life after School

The future is unhappened.

— Otis Dehann Carlyle

THERE IS LIFE AFTER SCHOOL, and students' visions of that life directly affect how hopeful they can be about their time in school. If they believe that school will make them more competent for that future, they will be motivated to learn. The curriculum in every class should have a direct bearing on life after school.

An example is the Steps to College program, a joint venture between Mission High School in San Francisco and San Francisco State University. High school students with long histories of failure take college preparatory courses after school and are given preference for acceptance into City College if they successfully pass the program. Students are paid a stipend for attending the afternoon class to compensate for wages lost by forgoing after-school jobs. To counter the students' negative attitudes about the possibilities of college helping "students like them" ("I can make more money selling drugs than whatever job I can get after college"), they are taken to places like McDonald's, not to see the burger flippers, but to see the managers. They discover that owning or managing a McDonald's pays as well as drug dealing without the risk of death or jail. They visit gas stations to see what happens in the office, not at the pumps. For these students, the view of local employment opportunities from a management perspective is a new concept. It makes a college degree far more attractive.

Another example, on a smaller scale, is part of a new program in the Santa Clara Schools. "Engineers from Silicon Valley's largest companies teach middle school students how geometry can lead to a career in building integrated circuits. In the process they hope to show youths that higher education and technical training are not just for nerds."[1]

All students face uncertain futures involving family, employment, and living in a local and a national community. Those who are at risk do not believe that America has gold-lined streets waiting for them after high school. "Since 1988, Toni Falbo of University of Texas at Austin and Harriett Romo of Southwest Texas State University have been tracking 100 Mexican-American teenagers. All the youngsters were labeled 'high risk' by their school district. As of last June, 40 percent had dropped out; Falbo predicts that an additional 20 percent will have quit by the time school starts next month."[2] The explanation offered for the high dropout rate of Mexican-American students by Frank Bean of UT at Austin is that the grandparents of this generation of Mexican-Americans believed in education and pushed it on their children as a means of getting ahead. But the next generation found no financial payoff. "The second generation, though better off than the first, loses that drive after getting stuck on welfare or in low paying jobs. They are more likely to give up and unlikely to push their own children as hard."[3]

Somehow, we must directly attack the hopelessness that pervades the perceptions of high risk students. They need dreams that have at least some chance to come true; and they need to see that education, while offering no guarantee, offers a reasonable chance to succeed. Here are some suggestions.

THE FAMILY

Ask teachers, administrators, social workers, child psychologists, juvenile judges, and the students themselves what is the biggest single reason for student failure in school, and their answer is "the breakdown of the family." Many children, and most of those who are at risk, have no role models for an effective family. Even many middle- and upper-class children do not live in homes that offer positive role models for parenting. Many financially advantaged children are being raised by absentee parents; they spend more time hanging out or with electronic baby sitters than with real people who offer real supervision. The most common source of a family picture is television. The best family role model on television is "The Cosby Show," but even that show gives the unrealistic expectation that all problems can be solved in 20 minutes.

If as many children in school come from dysfunctional families as the evidence suggests, then what does the future hold for their children when they become parents? The next generation of parents will consist of too many adults who have no idea of what a successful and fully functioning family can be.

If children are to have any hope for developing a meaningful family life, they need to see an effective family in operation. One way to give students the family skills they need and the role models they lack is to develop a course of study that begins in the first grade. Short modules on family living might be modeled after "Sesame Street," one television show that realistically portrays family life as a positive experience. The modules could include role-playing and game-playing activities that teach positive communication and conflict resolution. A family-living course is best a required part of the middle school and high school curriculum, and it should be given as much emphasis as English or math. These courses might include family training based on experiential activities. Students might examine different families' configurations; face family-type decisions and (through simulation) see how their decisions turn out; or role-play aspects of family life, such as living within a budget. They should examine why families fail and learn family-based communication skills to deal with potential failures. They should be taught parenting and discipline skills and learn how to have fun and pleasure within a family context. Courses like this already exist in a limited form in a small number of schools, but this concept should be expanded and required for all students. Students should learn how to become good parents.

Courses should be developed specifically for children who do not know what a successful family unit is. Preaching specific values must be avoided and replaced with a realistic assessment of the potential problems that threaten modern families. All family configurations should be legitimized and explored, including single-parent families, families with two working parents, and extended families with live-in grandparents.

The advance of technology has contributed to the separation of the oldest generation from the youngest. During earlier times and even now in many other countries, grandparents had a direct connection with children. The continuity between three (and sometimes four) generations provided security and a transition of culture, values, and spirit.

Children need to see that older people are not throwaway people. The older generations are a valuable and necessary natural resource. They have wisdom and patience and a history and love that exist nowhere else.

Schools cannot reunite grandparents with children at home, but they can provide a link with the older generation. Schools can connect formally with nursing homes, geriatric hospitals, apartment complexes and housing units for the elderly, and any other places where older people live. This connection might include sending middle school students to these places to help the elderly by reading to them, talking to them, playing games with them, even teaching them how to do a variety of things. In the process of helping, they will learn about values and about themselves and their valuable place in the world. The elderly can also teach about cooking, mending, building, creating cultural artwork, religion, and values. All students deserve the opportunity to benefit from earlier generations, at least once in middle school and once in high school.

Elderly people also should be brought into the school. They can sit in family-life classes and teach by telling stories, the way that history and culture was once so effectively taught. They can read to young children in the early grades; or they can be active in a variety of school functions such as aides, tutors, counselors, record keepers, or monitors. The elderly have accumulated knowledge and wisdom and have a love for children that is being wasted, thrown away needlessly.

The connection between the young and old is not a frivolous extra. How a society cares for its elderly reflects its values about hope and its future. Segregating the young from the old denies children an opportunity to form a positive perspective about the full range of their lives. When they get together, they learn from each other, respect each other, and care about each other. While not every child or elderly person can benefit from such a connection, most can.

Most importantly, the young and old provide hope for each other. Schools are in desperate need of hope. Why not take advantage of a potentially powerful resource that is mostly ignored?

PREPARING FOR JOBS

Without the hope for a job, students cannot realistically imagine having a successful family, or even imagine a reason to learn in school. Many of the jobs to which high risk students aspire are either unrealistic, extremely negative, dangerous, or illegal. Some students imagine themselves as rock or rap stars, major league ballplayers, or drug dealers. Each of these "professions" has the lure of fast money, requires no academic skills, and has highly visible role models who seem to have it made. But the percentage of people who actually make it in the arts or sports is infinitesimal compared to the number of people who try. The doors to most sports teams are closed to those without college experience.

Unfortunately, the only other options these students visualize is unemployment, flipping burgers, pumping gas, or some other relatively unappealing job. Unless students see other options, they will never have true hope for gainful employment. Every high school needs a program designed to encourage the possibility of some form of higher education or job training after graduation. The Steps to College plan described at the beginning of this chapter is one example of how to encourage students to think of going to college. In addition, schools need to connect with community resource teams to build links for jobs when students graduate.

Students should have inside tracks to employment based on their mastery of basic skills. Local merchants and larger companies have a stake in the employability of graduates, and they can do a lot by specifying what minimal competencies are required for their jobs and by guaranteeing employment to those who master these competencies. Students can spend a part of their school day in the business world, preparing for employment with on-the-job training. The stronger the connection between real jobs and school, the more the students will believe that employment is possible. If a diploma meant a job, less students would drop out.

Schools need to develop partnerships with large companies, and many schools have already done so. The businesses donate time, money, materials, and professional expertise to the school. The school provides educated students who will make good employees and good citizens. The more often these adoptions can include employment possibilities, the better.

All students, not just those with good grades, should understand that it is possible for them to get management positions and professional jobs. A vision of desirable employment is at least as important, if not more so, for those who are at risk in school and in life.

A good example of what schools can do to assist students in preparing for jobs and preparing teachers to include job skills in their courses is the MOIS program, developed by the Michigan State Board of Education. MOIS is a computerized system that analyzes thousands of jobs. Students can use MOIS to find out what jobs are available and what skills they need for each job. They can list jobs based on interests, areas of work, the physical strength required, the physical capabilities, the working conditions, required education, and the type of temperament best suited for the job. Teachers can use MOIS to find out how their courses relate to the requirements of various jobs in the state. Access to the system is widespread in secondary schools throughout the state. For example, every high school in Flint has access to the system. The more high risk students are encouraged to try the MOIS system, the greater the chance to encourage them to learn.

THE NEED FOR DEVELOPING HIGH-TECH SKILLS

All students need to learn how to use computers and other high-tech hardware and software before they graduate from high school, and the need increases every year. Students without high-tech skills will most likely find themselves unemployable. Students at risk especially need to be encouraged to develop high-tech skills.

I recommend that every school have a computer training program for their high risk students. Because working with computers is fun and motivational, it will do more than teach job skills; it has the potential to make school meaningful for students who are turned off to other subjects. Educators must be very careful to expand technical training for these students and not to let poor academic or behavior performance restrict its access. Computer training should never be considered a privilege or reward. Otherwise, the students who need it the most will get it the least. All programs to encourage high risk students to stay in school and develop a hopeful attitude should include a high-tech component.

LIVING IN A COMMUNITY

Communities at their best are interactive. Individuals give to the community, and the community supports the individual. This is true at the global, national, city, and neighborhood levels. However, the modern world has lost much of the sense of community. Neighborhoods in many cities are war zones: the suburbs are barren strongholds where citizens flock together for safety. Nationally, America is narrowing its areas of concern. States are fighting for economic and social control at the expense of the national good—for example, fighting over which military bases should close. Americans, fed up with the unresponsive nature of politicians, no longer vote. America has the lowest percentage of citizens who vote of any democracy. Apathy and hopelessness are pervasive.

Once again, the question is what schools can or should do to deal with these issues. My answer is that schools should do whatever they can to help, because every means for giving hope to students is in the best interest of the school. The more hopeful students are about their life after school, the more they will be willing to put energy into school.

There is not a great deal that can be done to convince students that they as individuals can change national social policies and the economic conditions that affect them. However, they can learn that voting is at least a step in the right direction. Every vote lost by the disenfranchised gives more power to those who disenfranchise them. Even MTV had a drive to convince eighteen-year-olds to vote in the 1988 presidential election. Starting from the early grades, classes in social studies should begin stressing the need for everyone to vote. The concept of empowerment should be discussed regularly, along with the notion that politicians actually listen to groups who represent blocks of votes when elections are at stake. Mock elections can occur every year, beginning in first grade through high school. Elections should occur both in the classroom and schoolwide. Voting should be a natural way of life for most students by the time they leave high school.

High school students need to learn how to register, how to operate voting machines, and how to fill out absentee ballots. These are the tools of democracy, and every citizen must have them. During each election year, registration can occur at the high school for those old enough to vote. Others can watch the registration process in action so that it is demystified.

Debating issues that affect national policy should begin early. History classes can include examples of voter groups who swung elections. Big deals should be made over the enfranchisement of women and blacks, not only as events but as cultural revolutions. Students should be confronted every year with information about how important it is for them to vote.

It is easier to show students how they can make a difference in their community. Community groups throughout the country are reclaiming neighborhoods; they are fighting drug dealers, finding shelters for the homeless, and discovering political power. In San Francisco, every neighborhood has a group that lobbies City Hall for improvements and that has a strong influence regarding such neighborhood regulations as zoning, law enforcement, and housing.

These groups can become liaisons between neighborhoods and children. Devote part of the school week to a "neighborhood studies curriculum" that examines how residents can improve neighborhoods. On a regular basis, bring to school such community resource people as social workers, store owners, police, religious leaders, storefront community groups, and those who fight homelessness, drug abuse, and AIDS both professionally and out of personal dedication. Teach children that the community matters and that neighborhoods can be reclaimed.

School also might become a rallying point for adults who want to reclaim their neighborhoods. The local PTA/PTO groups can identify and develop community action programs. Once again, such local agencies as the police, social workers, and business can begin to work together to rebuild safer, more livable neighborhoods. What better metaphor for hope could children see?

As I said in the beginning of this chapter, school cannot significantly change the lives children face outside of school. Schools can, however, directly provide the attitudes and skills necessary for those changes to occur. Most importantly, schools can offer hope that changes are possible and worth fighting for.

---

1. Turner, Dan, "Engineers get a Chance to Turn Kids on to Math," *San Francisco Chronicle,* 14 October 1991, p. A 16.

2. Kantrowitz, Barbara and Rosado, Lourdes, "Falling Further Behind," *Newsweek Magazine,* 19 August 19 1991, p. 60.

3. Ibid, p. 60.

Fifteen

Conclusion

I T IS THE BEGINNING OF ANOTHER SCHOOL DAY and students are streaming into the halls in what at first appears to be random, chaotic patterns. They come in all shapes, sizes, and colors, wearing every imaginable style of clothing. Some are hurrying to their classrooms, others to meet their boy or girl friends. Most seem to be traveling at warp speed, even if they do not seem to be going anywhere. Today will be just like yesterday and just like tomorrow.

Even a casual glance at their faces reveals a total emotional range. Some are rehearsing their class assignments or practicing for their tests. Some are rehearsing their excuses and practicing their explanations of why they are not ready. Some of them are a million miles from school, wondering if everyone in their family will be alive when they get home.

The pattern, as chaotic and random as it seems, soon dissolves into classes with each student sitting in a pre-established seat, behaving in a pre-established manner, doing pre-established tasks. Statistics can predict with accuracy the number of students who will leave that day feeling successful, the number of students who will be thrown out of the class to the principal's office, the number of students who will fail.

But what if tomorrow was not like today? What if one teacher, one administrator, one entire school faculty, or one campus decided to organize the chaos into a new pattern, one that was no longer predictable day-after-day drudgery, especially for those students who come to school without hope? What if that school committed itself to positively influencing all of their lives? What if something intervened? What if someone said, "You no longer have to fail. You can make a positive difference. You have reason to hope. Your life and your existence are important to us,"? What if it were your school?

What would happen then?

Bibliography

Ackerman, P. (1971). "The Effect of Honor Grading on Students' Test Scores." *American Educational Research Journal* 8, 2: 321-333.

Anno, M. (1977). *Anno's Journey*. New York: Philomel Books.

Ashton-Warner, S. (1963). *Teacher*. New York: Simon & Schuster.

Berman, C. (1991). *Adult Children of Divorce Speak Out*. New York: Simon & Schuster.

Berne, E. (1964). *Games People Play*. New York: Grove Press.

Black, S. (1991). "Self-Esteem and Nonsense." *The American School Board Journal* 178, 7: 27-29.

Blankstein, A. (1992). "Lessons from Enlightened Corporations." *Educational Leadership* 49, 6: 71-75.

Boyer, E. (1983). *High School: A Report on Secondary Education in America*. New York: Harper Colophon.

Braddock, J. (1990). "Tracking the Middle Grades: National Patterns of Grouping for Instruction." *Phi Delta Kappan* 71, 6: 445-449.

Brendtro, L., Brokenleg, M., and Van Bockern, S. (1990). *Reclaiming Youth At Risk: Our Hope for the Future*. Bloomington, IN: National Educational Service.

Castendeda, C. (1971). *A Separate Reality*. New York: Pocket Books.

Cohn, A. (1990). "Tracking Derailed." *Parenting Magazine* September: 40.

Csikszentmihalyi, M. (1990). *Flow: The Psychology of Optimal Experience.* New York: Harper and Row.

Curwin, R. (1980). "Are Your Students Addicted to Praise?" *Instructor* 90, 3: 61-62.

Curwin, R. (1990). *Entering Adulthood: Teaching Student Responsibility and Self-Discipline.* Network Publications.

Curwin, R. and Fuhrmann, B. (1975). *Discovering Your Teaching Self: Humanistic Approaches to Effective Teaching.* Englewood Cliffs, NJ: Prentice-Hall.

Curwin, R., Fuhrmann, B., and Demart, P. (1988). *Making Evaluation Meaningful.* New York: Irvington Press.

Curwin, R. and Mendler, A. (1980). *The Discipline Book: A Complete Guide to School and Classroom Management.* Reston, VA: Reston Publishing Co.

Curwin, R. and Mendler, A. (1988). *Discipline With Dignity.* Alexandria, VA: Association for Supervision and Curriculum Development.

Curwin, R. and Mendler, A. (1990). *Am I In Trouble?: Using Discipline to Teach Young Children Responsibility.* Network Publications.

Deming, W.E. (1988) *Out of the Crisis.* Cambridge, MA: MIT Press.

Doyle, R. (1989). "The Resistance of Conventional Wisdom to Research Evidence: The Case of Retention in Grade." *Phi Delta Kappan* 71, 3: 215-220.

Driekurs, R. (1964). *Children: The Challenge.* New York: Hawthorn Books.

Firestone, W. (1989). "Beyond Order and Expectations in High Schools Serving At-Risk Youth." *Educational Leadership* 46, 5: 41-45.

Frankl, V. (1963). *Man's Search For Meaning: An Introduction to Logotherapy.* New York: Pocket Books.

Frymier, J. and Gansneder, B. (1989). "The Phi Delta Kappa Study of Students At Risk." *Phi Delta Kappan* 71, 2: 142-146.

Frymier, J. (1985). *Motivation to Learn.* Bloomington, IN: Phi Delta Kappa.

Giffon and Patton (1974). *Personal Communications in Human Relations.* Columbus, OH: Merrill.

Glasser, W. (1990). "The Quality School." *Phi Delta Kappan* 71, 6: 424-435.

Hembree, D. (1989). "The Tragic Side of Classroom Punishment." *Hippocrates* March/April: 116.

Hicks, B. (1990). *Youth Suicide: A Comprehensive Manual for Prevention and Intervention.* Bloomington, IN: National Educational Service.

Kantor, A. (1987). *The Book of Alfred Kantor: An Artist's Journal of the Holocaust.* New York: Schocken Books.

Lewis, A. (1990). "Washington Commentary: Tracking and the National Goals." *Phi Delta Kappan* 72, 2: 100-107.

Malouf, D. (1983). "Do Rewards Reduce Student Motivation?" *School Psychology Review* 12, 1: 1-11.

Maslow, A. (1962). *Toward a Psychology of Being.* Princeton, NJ: Van Nostrand.

Maslow, A. (1965). *Eupsychian Management: A Journal.* Homewood, IL: Irwin-Dorsey.

May, R. (1969). *Love and Will.* New York: Norton.

Mendler, A. (1992). *What Do I Do When...? How to Achieve Discipline With Dignity in the Classroom.* Bloomington, IN: National Educational Service.

Mendler, A. and Curwin, R. (1983). *Taking Charge in the Classroom.* Reston, VA: Reston Publishing Co.

Mendler, A. (1990). *Smiling at Yourself: Educating Young Children about Stress and Self-Esteem.* Network Publishing Co.

Molnar, A. (1989). "Racism in America: A Continuing Dilemma." *Educational Leadership* 47, 2: 71-72.

Molnar, A. and Linquist, B. (1990). *Changing Problem Behavior in Schools.* San Francisco: Jossey-Bass.

Patterson, J. and Peter, K. (1991). *The Day America Spoke The Truth.* Englewood Cliffs, NJ: Prentice-Hall.

Rogers, C. (1969). *Freedom to Learn.* Columbus, OH: Merrill.

Rosenthal, R. and Jacobsen, L. (1969). *Pygmalion in the Classroom: Self-Fulfilling Prophecies and Teacher Expectations.* New York: Holt, Rinehart, Winston.

Salinger, J.D. (1953). "Teddy." *Nine Stories.* New York: Bantam Books.

Shepard, L. and Smith, M. (1990). "Synthesis of Research on Grade Retention." *Educational Leadership* 47, 8: 84-88.

Starch and Elliot. *School Review.* 1921, 20: 442-445; 1913, 21: 254-259.

Sikula, J. (1986). "Visions of Reform: Implications for the Education Profession." Report of the ATE Blue Ribbon Task Force, Reston, VA.

Strong, L. (1989). "The Best Kids They Have." *Educational Leadership* February.

Wyatt, S. (nd). *The Mark: A Case for the Abolition of Grading.* Washington, DC: Center for Educational Reform.

Wlodkowski, R. (1978). *Motivation and Teaching.* Washington, DC: National Education Association.

Wlodkowski, R. and Jarnes, J. (1990). *Eager to Learn.* San Francisco: Jossey-Bass.

About *Rediscovering Hope: Our Greatest Teaching Strategy* and the National Educational Service

The mission of the National Educational Service is to provide tested and proven resources that help those who work with youth create safe and caring schools, agencies, and communities where all children succeed. *Rediscovering Hope: Our Greatest Teaching Strategy* is just one of many resources and staff development opportunities NES provides that focus on building a community circle of caring. If you have any questions, comments, articles, manuscripts, or youth art you would like us to consider for publication, please contact us at the address below. Or visit our website at:

www.nesonline.com

Staff Development Opportunities Include:

Improving Schools through Quality Leadership
Integrating Technology Effectively
Creating Professional Learning Communities
Building Cultural Bridges
Discipline with Dignity
Ensuring Safe Schools
Managing Disruptive Behavior
Reclaiming Youth At Risk
Working with Today's Families

National Educational Service
304 West Kirkwood Avenue, Suite 2
Bloomington, IN 47404-5132
(812) 336-7700
(800) 733-6786 (toll-free number)
FAX (812) 336-7790
e-mail: nes@nesonline.com
www.nesonline.com

NEED MORE COPIES OR ADDITIONAL RESOURCES ON THIS TOPIC?

Need more copies of this book? Want your own copy? Need additional resources on this topic? If so, you can order additional materials by using this form or by calling us toll free at (800) 733-6786 or (812) 336-7700. Or you can order by FAX at (812) 336-7790, or visit our website at www.nesonline.com.

Title	Price*	Quantity	Total
Rediscovering Hope: Our Greatest Teaching Strategy	$ 21.95		
Discipline with Dignity for Challenging Youth	24.95		
What Do I Do When . . . ? How to Achieve Discipline with Dignity	21.95		
Power Struggles	11.95		
Discipline with Dignity Video Set	356.00		
As Tough as Necessary Video Set	395.00		
Lessons for Life: How Smart Schools Boost Academic, Social, and Emotional Intelligence Video Set	495.00		
An Educator's Legal Guide to Stress-Free Discipline and School Safety	79.00		
Anger Management for Youth: Stemming Aggression and Violence	24.95		
Teaching Self-Control: A Curriculum for Responsible Behavior	27.95		
		SUBTOTAL	
		SHIPPING	
Please add 6% of order total. For orders outside the continental U.S., please add 8% of order total.			
		HANDLING	
Please add $4. For orders outside the continental U.S., please add $6.			
		TOTAL (U.S. funds)	

*Price subject to change without notice.

❑ Check enclosed   ❑ Purchase order enclosed
❑ Money order   ❑ VISA, MasterCard, Discover, or American Express (circle one)

Credit Card No._____ Exp. Date_____
Cardholder Signature _____

Ship to:
First Name_____ Last Name_____
Position _____
Institution Name_____
Address_____
City_____ State_____ ZIP_____
Phone_____ FAX_____
E-mail _____

National Educational Service
304 West Kirkwood Avenue, Suite 2
Bloomington, IN 47404-5132
(812) 336-7700 • (800) 733-6786 (toll-free number)
FAX (812) 336-7790
e-mail: nes@nesonline.com • www.nesonline.com